K. Spain

Blessing New Voices

Prayers of Young People
and Worship Resources for
Youth Ministry

Maren C. Tirabassi

UNITED CHURCH PRESS   CLEVELAND, OHIO

United Church Press, Cleveland, Ohio 44115
© 2000 by Maren C. Tirabassi

Biblical quotations, unless otherwise noted, are from the New Revised
Standard Version of the Bible, © 1989 by the Division of Christian Education
of the National Council of Churches of Christ in the U.S.A., and are used
by permission. Adaptations have been made for inclusivity.

Printed in the United States of America on acid-free paper

05   04   03   02   01   00   5   4   3   2   1

Library of Congress Cataloging-in-Publication Data

Tirabassi, Maren C.
    Blessing new voices : prayers of young people and worship resources
for youth ministry / Maren C. Tirabassi.
        p.   cm.
    ISBN 0-8298-1402-7 (pbk. : alk. paper)
    1. Church work with youth—United Church of Christ.   2. Worship
programs.   3. Prayers.   I. Title.

BV4447 .T57 2000
264'.05834'00835—dc21

                                                    00-036451

contents

foreword

Maren C. Tirabassi and her many youthful co-writers have done something wonderfully unusual in *Blessing New Voices*. They have put together a youth ministry resource which is "nuts and bolts practical" (the kind of book you can grab when you've either procrastinated or been too busy, and count on to provide you with something you can use in *tonight's* youth group meeting!), and yet also inspiring and personally moving (the kind of book you might turn to for personal devotional reading, or draw from in a time of crisis).

It is obvious from Maren's contributions to this work that she has been ministering to and with young people for a long time. She understands teenagers—the emotional flow and rhythm of the school year, the hot button personal issues which often swell to overwhelming proportions during adolescence, and the bittersweet groping for meaning and purpose which so many teens experience and often agonize over. Maren has an amazing gift for using symbols and creating exercises and liturgies which invite teenagers to bring their whole, *real* selves into the processes of spiritual journeying and faith exploration. Without being overly "preachy" or "churchy," these activities help students explore, experience, and express deep spiritual content in an atmosphere of loving affirmation and Christian community. Perhaps Maren's greatest contribution is her ability to help young people experience the joy and the tears of heartfelt worship. The liturgies for worship in *Blessing New Voices* are not just about putting already written liturgical words into the mouths of teenagers; these liturgies help teens find and share their own faith, their own ways of meeting and knowing the God of the Bible, and their own words and ways of praying.

I think Maren would be the first to concur that the "best" this book has to offer comes from the young people who risked offering their prayers for publication in this resource. I enthusiastically applaud Maren's choice to include prayers from every person who was willing to submit them. This was no contest to see who could write the "best" prayers; God knows our young people experience more than enough competition in just about every aspect of their lives. This book is a powerful reminder to the youth of our congregations (and to the church at large) that there are no right or wrong ways to pray. There are no bad prayers. To be sure, we can and perhaps should wrestle with the theological content of the prayers we read and hear and pray, but this book is more a celebration of *in*tent than an analysis of *content*— and rightly so in my opinion.

In terms of content, style, theology, language, length, and tone, these prayers are "all over the place"—and I'm glad they are. The teenage years are "all over the place." For that matter, life for most of us is "all over the place," and it seems only appropriate that our prayers reflect this wide range of emotion and experience. There is wonderful diversity in just about every possible way in the offerings of these young writers. As one who has spent an almost frightening amount of time hanging out with teenagers in the context of my musical ministry, reading the prayers of *Blessing New Voices* was like being surrounded by a familiar cloud of witnesses. I heard the beautiful voices of many young lives I've been privileged to reach out to in retreats and concerts over the years. But they were reaching out to me this time—challenging me with their questions and viewpoints, inviting me into deeper understanding of their teenage world, refreshing me with their rawness and blunt honesty, comforting me with their deep faith, reminding me of what I know and believe but sometimes forget, entertaining and inspiring me through the artistic soulfulness of their poetry, and taking me deeper into the very heart of God. I laughed, I cried, I felt touched by the Holy Spirit, and I was overwhelmed with gratitude to God for blessing the church with these young ministers.

Finally, I have a hunch that the prayers in this book will help many more teenagers realize that they too have the capacity to pray in their own personal style and words, and that the church not only wants to hear and share these prayers, but longs to be led in worship by its young people. May this book serve as a powerful affirmation of the contributions teenagers and young adults have to make to the church's present, and may it encourage more and more young people to share their much needed and deeply appreciated gifts with the broader church community.

BRYAN C. SIRCHIO

introduction
listening to the voices

 In the spring of 1998, several events converged which led to this book. I spent an April Saturday teaching poetry at the New Hampshire Young Writers' Conference, an annual event that gathers more than one hundred teenagers to share their fiction, poetry, and essays and to learn from one another and from professional writers. I was struck by the students' incredible gifts for clothing their feelings with language and by their listening to one another rather than being competitive, which is what the high school environment often fosters. These young people were excited by one another's words.

Then, in May, I took my youth group from rural Northwood, New Hampshire, to New York City. At the Bowery Mission they fed homeless people and then took a converted paddy wagon to street corners, where they handed out cardboard bowls of soup and distributed religious tracts (not a typical U.C.C. activity!!). When we came together in the worship circle, I could see that there was a lot on their minds and in their hearts, so I gave them index cards and asked them to write prayers and then redistribute them, so that everyone would be reading aloud someone else's prayer. These young people had seen, felt, and "theologized" far more than I could have imagined.

Only a week later, Joan Jordan Grant and I were giving a reading and presentation from our book, *An Improbable Gift of Blessing*. Two middle-school students, Liana Merrill and Gabriele Chase, sat in the front row. When we opened the floor for questions, one of them asked, "Where are the prayers for us? Where are the prayers for kids?"

And so, Gabe and Liana, here are the prayers. It's taken two years and more than one hundred sixty writers between the ages of twelve and twenty-one to bring it off, but *Blessing New Voices: Prayers of Young People and Worship Resources for Youth Ministry* is my response to you.

Half of this book—the more important half—is an anthology of prayers. I led workshops with young people, sent flyers to conference offices, logged hundreds of phone hours, and made more announcements at clergy, Christian education, youth ministry, and outdoor ministry meetings than were probably welcome. My personal commitment was to create a forum in which the voices of young adults could be heard and valued, not as the "future of the church" but as a vibrant present reality. This was not a contest! Far too much of the environment that young people live and work in is shaped by scores and grades. *Blessing New Voices* is a project of cooperation, collaboration, and inclusion.

Young people responded. They wrote with spiritual authority, compassion, and sensitivity. Coming from fifteen states, the writers represent the diversity of the United Church of Christ. I am particularly appreciative of those I have worked with from different traditions, both Christian denominations and other families of faith. Although this is essentially a Christian book, its pages are honored, indeed graced, by its guests from other faith traditions.

WORSHIPING WITH YOUTH

The other half of *Blessing New Voices* consists of worship resources for youth ministry. In the same season as Liana and Gabe's challenge, I was hired by the Massachusetts Conference to teach "Creative Worship for Youth." The class was excited. They reported that although music, games, mission ideas, and discussion starters are abundant, youth group worship plans are rare. Each chapter that follows has a youth ministry activity and a worship service coordinated with prayers submitted on the theme. These eleven chapters roughly correspond to programming that begins in September and concludes with a combined July and August youth group session, "Celebrating the Earth."

Some of these ideas in different adaptations have appeared in *Church Worship Magazine*, in *Re-Imagining: Quarterly Publication of the Re-Imagining Community*, and as part of a worship resource with Bryan Sirchio's song "The Table of Friendship and Love," found on his compact disc *The Artist's Hand*.

Young people are a people of worship. Their shared reflections and ritual activities are often worshipful, whether the name of the context is "church" or not. I would like to pause before the "real" beginning of this book, "Opening Doors," to offer a rationale for youth ministry worship and share some of its important elements.

Worshiping with Youth—Whys

Adolescence is often the age at which young people are thrust out of a "children's sermon" and "junior church" context into adult Sunday services, as if somehow the skills and the desire for such services were naturally acquired at that time. Religious puberty is exciting, needy, and wonderful, as those engaged in confirmation programs can attest. Responding to this age and stage with only mandatory adult Sunday service attendance often results in a ten-year leave of absence from the church. Complementing congregational worship with services focused on the concerns of youth and frequently shaped and led by young people acknowledges the transition and creates a more dynamic faith community because of it.

Worship exists for the sake of worship. It is not a teaching tool, though many things are learned in its embrace; it is not a performance by singers or speakers or dancers or instrumentalists, although many gifts artistically prepared are enthusiastically appreciated; it is neither a persuader nor a pacifier, although history gives evidence that worship has at times been used to oppress people. Worship is for the sake of worship—it is for God's sake and for the human sake of sharing tears and laughter.

Worship takes place in the midst of congregation. Most other contemporary group activities are based in "audience." A select group of participants—athletes, actors, lecturers, musicians—present their work, while a larger group passively receive it. This is not a bad thing. From Broadway to the Little League field, this is an exciting way of sharing talents. But, just because this kind of presentation is so common, it is important to distinguish for young people that in worship all participants are active. Worship is not something that one "gets something out of," but an opportunity for giving.

Another reason for worship in a youth ministry context is to develop a love of worship, an understanding of the rhythm of worship, and the skills for self-expression in worship. Perfunctory devotional moments, grace before meals, and songfests without interpretation and reflection are not enough to root worship in a person's life. However, if once or twice a month a young person opens to communal prayer and wrestles with scripture in a non-threatening environment, the desire for such a graced experience will grow.

People bring prayers—for themselves and for others—to worship. Prayer, too, is learned and deepened in practice. Prayer is not a "answer-finding" enterprise—there is no diagnosis, as in medicine, or verdict, as in law. It isn't the lottery, where a winning number is drawn, or a book/movie/CD waiting for a review. In an acceptably unfinished way prayer lifts up hope, doubt, fear, joy, sorrow, wonder. These feelings, in their full, indecisive beauty, are the landscape of adolescent life.

Finally, worship is the anticipation and experience of meaningful encounters with God, encounters that change lives. In contemporary society, holy expectation is often a solitary activity. Worship provides the time and place for sharing private epiphanies and affirming a community of revelation.

Worshiping with Youth—How-To's

The most important element in designing effective and dynamic worship with young adults is providing a variety of easy, safe opportunities to participate. Circles of conversation have a baseline of brief response—such as saying one's name—but also the possibility of telling a story and deciding how much to risk in the telling. Other helpful methods to structure a supportive environment include a choice between spoken, written, or artistic response, and a choice between sharing with a partner or triad or engaging the full group.

Each year is a universe for young people. The school calendar recognizes this with homecomings, proms, banquets, and graduations. Youth ministry needs to reflect seasonal dimensions. In addition there is an annual rhythm of high autumn energy, deepening community through the winter and spring months, and then a release beginning in late spring as the program year ends and relationships need to be renegotiated.

Adolescence is a highly charged physical time. Requiring young people to hug or even hold hands can create intense discomfort. Passing an object, such as a candle, a crocus bulb, or a rock offers connection without anxiety. Requiring a danced response can be almost unbearable for some young people. Having rhythm instruments as an alternative allows those people to find a comfort level without calling attention to themselves.

Contemporary experience is silence-deprived. Worship is deepened by silence, but developing skill in absorbing silence requires gradually increasing exposure to it. Young people are also starved for sensory data because so much information exchange is "screened." Worship that involves tactile sensations and stimulates the senses of smell and taste is powerful because these senses are underused. Even church services are experienced as dominated by hearing. Effective worship with youth is rooted in parable and sacrament to engage the whole person.

Youth ministry needs to be language-inclusive, modeling the freshest, clearest, and most affirming language the faith community can sing, shout, whisper. Young people are offended by images of sin as blind or black, or divinity as male or master. Nevertheless, being criticized for the language one uses in prayer can be a faith-shattering experience. Sometimes churches in the United Church of Christ undermine the fragile-heartfelt with the thoughtless-correct.

Finally, youth ministry worship needs to be real. Honesty and authenticity cover multiple faults. Youth ministry worship can be the place where individuals bring the problems of family, school and relationships. It is also the place where concerns about justice and natural disasters, ethical dilemmas, and fears about the future can be placed in the hands of grace.

SOME PERSONAL BLESSINGS

I wish to express thanks to leaders who have worked with groups of young people in creating or soliciting prayers—David Pendleton, Rosemary McCombs Maxey, Oscar Brockmeyer, Susan Campbell, Jeff Puhlmann-Becker, Russ Harlow, Tony Acheson, Kathy Johntra, Anne Jackson, Cindy Stahler, Judith Brain, Sharon Graff, Linda Hillyer, Cheryl Smith, Jane Hess, Molly Phinney, Carl McDonald, and Ellen Fineberg and other staff from Temple Israel.

I am also grateful to Gordon Svoboda for his assistance in promotion and at General Synod; to Peter Johnston, who created the flyer that tempted so many young people to write prayers; to Gregg Pitman, my window to outdoor ministries; to Bryan Sirchio for his gracious foreword; and to Kim Sadler and the wonderful staff of United Church Press for making this book possible and my work easy in so many ways.

I am always grateful to my family for their gift of time, support, and emotional hand-holding as I work on books. My husband, Donald, has given this project a huge donation of patience. Beyond all others I am grateful to my children. Maria's insightful writing and priceless administrative assistance and Matthew's artistic advice and encouragement have truly shaped *Blessing New Voices*.

1 opening doors

The beginning of the youth ministry program year is a challenging time when new people are integrated into the ongoing group. That may include a younger grade and newcomers to the community, as well as perhaps youth attracted by an intentional effort to reach out to young people inside and outside the church membership who have not previously been engaged in the youth group. Welcoming diversity and encouraging new ideas and leadership are important. In addition, all the young people are facing the challenges of a new school year, new activities, and sometimes new friends and new jobs. They are opening doors.

YOUTH MINISTRY ACTIVITY

Gather around a table covered with white paper. Have a basket, a large, "clocky"-looking alarm clock, and a variety of different-colored ink pads, pencils, and wet wipes on the table. Pass the basket for an "offering" of watches. (Assure them that they can retrieve the watches later.) Time may be the most valuable thing adolescents have. Their time is claimed by school, activities, sports, friends, family, and jobs. To come to a youth group meeting should be honored as a gift of time. The leader or leadership team may want to make a statement of commitment to honor the time given, and to suggest that the youth group members pledge to be faithful to one another in not wasting one another's time or the preparation time of leaders.

Pass the alarm clock around the circle, having each person say, "This year I want to have time in my life for _____." Expand this wish beyond the church community, to include what is most pressing for each member in his or her life

Discuss the individuality of fingerprints and the uniqueness of each person. Invite each participant to put ten fingerprints on the white paper covering the table. They can use different colors and make a design or simply repeat one print ten times. Suggest that they write beside each print a personal characteristic, talent, or interest (for example— sister, shy, blond, tennis, sci-fi novels, etc.). Go around the circle and have each person share aloud three of the characteristics. Then play a couple of rounds of "musical chairs" without removing a chair each time and have the youth sit down and try to identify whose fingerprints are at each place.

If there is additional time, the group can design a banner celebrating the beginning of the youth ministry year for the following week in church using only fingerprints.

Closing Prayer

Gentle God, we give you thanks for the holy difference
and the precious gifts in each of us.
Receive the offerings of our individuality,
for we pledge that our fingerprints
will always be found on open hands. Amen.

WORSHIP SERVICE

This service takes place in an informal circle with soft light and a spacious low table with a cloth on it to hold the objects that will be passed around. There are ten objects on the table—a small pitcher of water, a bowl of ashes, a cruse of sweet-smelling oil, a dish of salt, a candle in a glass lantern to make it easy to see and handle, a rock, a towel, a loaf of bread, a cup of grape juice, and a basket with enough old keys that each participant can take one away.

Ten people should be given scripture in advance, or it can be marked and placed under chairs. The form of the service is the reading of a text and then a sentence of direction from the leader, as the objects are passed from hand to hand around the circle. Some of the objects listed above can be deleted to shorten the service. During the passing, hymns familiar enough that they do not need to be read or accompanied can be sung. Suggestions are: "Amazing Grace," "Kumbaya," "Lord, I Want to Be a Christian," "This Little Light of Mine," "Give Me Oil in My Lamp" (softly), "Amen," "Alleluia," "Let Us Break Bread Together."

Call to Worship

During the course of this youth ministry year together many things will happen. We celebrate the fact that common, everyday experiences—car washes and pancake breakfasts, overnights and games and movies and silly jokes retold again and again—will be special, in fact will be "holy" for us. Jesus told stories using common things that his listeners experienced every day. He "parabled" these objects. During this year we will often do the same thing with objects familiar to us—use them as metaphors for our deepest feelings. Today (tonight) we will begin by looking at some of the metaphors from scripture, ones we often read about but rarely see, touch, taste, or smell, and we will do so praying that these old metaphors may make new meanings for us.

Someone has a scripture about water.

Water: John 4:7–15

As we pass this pitcher we remember the Red Sea, the Jordan River, perhaps your own baptism, the living water of Jesus Christ, and the fact that we are mostly made of water. When you receive the pitcher, put a drop of water on your forehead if you wish.

Someone has a scripture about ashes.

Ashes: Jonah 3

Ashes have always been a sign of regret, sorrow, and willingness to begin again. We are never perfect! When you receive the ashes, mark a spot on the back of your hand with them if you wish.

Someone has a scripture about oil.

Oil: Psalm 45:6–7; Isaiah 61:1–3

We are a people of ashes and oil, repentance and gladness. Oil is a symbol of fun, and we *will* have fun this year! As we pass the oil, place a drop near the ashes reminding you of the sheer joy of our good news.

Someone has a scripture about rock.

Rock: Matthew 7:24–27

Feel the weight of this rock. Think about stability, but also remember that stones have been used to wound and kill. God places a rock in our hands—the choice is ours to build on it a strong youth ministry or to throw it at someone.

Someone has a scripture about salt.

Salt: Matthew 5:13–16

Salt is a symbol of the hidden faithfulness in our lives as Christians. Put a little salt on your tongue. Taste it and remember there are many ways to be faithful—at home, at school, at work—without calling attention to yourself.

Someone has a scripture about light.

Light: John 1:1–5

We are lights in the world as we reflect the Light of the World. As we pass the candle, let the light shine into your life. If there are people you would like us all to hold in prayer, please name them when you have the candle. You may say why you want to pray for them, simply mention a name, or hold the name silently in our prayerful attention.

Someone has a scripture about a towel.

Towel: John 13:1–15

As we pass this towel, let us commit ourselves to following Jesus' loving example. When you hold the towel, think of one way you could serve someone else.

Let us pray: Gracious God, the metaphors to which we turn now are different from those which have gone before. We remember that on Jesus' last Passover evening with his disciples he broke bread and gave it to them as an anticipation of his body being broken, and he poured a cup and prayed and offered it as a new covenant for the forgiveness of sin. As we remember, we too break bread and pour a holy cup to the end that our hearts are healed, our spirits renewed, and our lives filled with your life. Send your Spirit, O God, that this bread may be sacred and the cup filled with blessing. Amen.

Someone has a scripture about bread.

Bread: Luke 22:14–20

Let us pass this bread in faith and love, each saying to our neighbor, "The gift of Christ for you." Hold the bread in your hand and then we will share the cup by intinction.

Someone has a scripture about the cup.

Cup: 1 Corinthians 11:23–26

Let us pass this cup, holding it for one another to dip the bread, saying, "This is the cup of blessing,"

Three of you have scripture about Opening Doors.

Opening Doors: Matthew 7:7–8; John 14:1–3, Revelation 3:20

We have come to the beginning of our youth ministry year together. We are opening the door to many experiences, to new faces and possibilities. Each one of us will have some moments of uncertainty during the year as we face choices between different doors. As a symbol of this special time, we are going to pass a basket of keys. Choose one to take home and hang on a string somewhere you can see often. Each person offer the basket to the next one and say, "I give you a key and Christ opens the door."

Let us pray: Gracious God, this broken bread brings us healing; this cup gives us life; and these precious symbols of water and ashes, oil and rock, salt and light, towel, and key make your words more real in our lives. We thank you for your presence as metaphor and reality. Amen.

Benediction

We have passed around many things this afternoon (evening). Now we pass the most precious and fragile thing of all—Christ's peace and our mutual blessing.

The peace of Christ be with you.

And also with you.

prayers by young people

OPENING DOORS

Dear God,
the key to the locked door
is within You,
and the door reveals colorful
animals, people, and all other creatures
on the earth we know and love.

The door reveals the earth
with peace and harmony,
colored with crayons when,
as not today,
no one minds if anyone clashes.

O Holy God, help us to pray
that we might understand our similarities
and differences.
Amen.

Jessica McCabe

God, open the doors of wonder which we see every day, but rarely
venture past. Let us be daring and bold. Help us do something dangerous every day of our lives, for what is life without adventure?
Open different windows—so we see something we have never seen,
think of things we have never thought of before, reach for something
that we have never felt. Guide us through the doors that we open but
then our minds want to scuttle back, shut, and be safe. Don't let us
pass by the doors of wonder. Amen.

Kathy Garlo

I See My Reflection through Jesus' Eyes

Eyes so kind,
Eyes so gentle,
Eyes so full of love.

Through these eyes, I see my reflection

Eyes so compassionate,
Eyes so forgiving,
Eyes so full of love.

Through these eyes, I see my reflection

Eyes so healing,
Eyes so peaceful,
Eyes so forever full of love.

Through these eyes, I see my reflection

In these eyes I see the power of God's love,
I see eyes so calm and understanding
Eyes so warm with strength to embrace
The whole earth with their eternal grace

Through these eyes, I see my reflection

Laura Aldorisio

Dear God
Help us see what we saw through your eyes. In the children of
poverty playing in the dust help us to realize that it isn't wealth that
makes us happy. We see ourselves in these children from their games:
hopscotch, clapping games, soccer in the dust. We can join with them.

Dear God, help us to know that faith, the belief in you, is what
makes the people there strong. And, as with the games, help us to know
that we, too, can join in. Even though we felt our faith was shallow in
comparison with the people of Mexico, they are our brothers and sisters, no better or worse, and through you we have all been found.

*(Written after a mission trip to Mazatlán, Mexico, by members of First
Congregational Church, United Church of Christ, Corvallis, Oregon)*

Mary Beth Budd, Andrea Mueller-Warrant

Bastet. Virgin; Woman of light; Dark Goddess;
Aphrodite; Earth Mother; Sister Sky; Maiden-
Mother-Crone; and all other deities, from
the Sun and Moon and deepest Earth,
those who have gone before and those who
will come after, borne on sand and wind
and wave, come to me. If all women are
blessed and all Goddesses one, teach me
to love and live and recognize truth and
to be thankful. Show me how to see evil,
to understand and recognize and to help and
share. Help me live for the past and future
and here and now, the night and day and what
comes beyond that, for the pulsing tides and
the endless wheel, and for the earth and planet
which I in part own, in part make, and in
part am made of. Bless me and teach me
and love me, as I am. For you of whom
the impossible is demanded, and from whom
the impossible is granted, let me in turn
bless You, and teach You, and love You,
　　You who created love.

Jessie Bellantone

God, grant me the willpower to not be afraid of who I am. I have
been through so much I am confident you can help me. Bring me to
see that I am someone and I am worth living for. Amen.

Maria

I am
an individual,
a person; no, a gift from God,
born into this world to bring joy and happiness
to the lives of those who dare not expect it
in theirs.

May the Lord above forgive my sins and temptations
that lie in my pathway to the future . . .
because I could not bear the shun of that
almighty shoulder turned away from me,
if not for Jesus,
and the loving, forgiving, tender heart
he inherited from God.

It is so true and yet so misunderstood
that Jesus, King of Kings,
died for all the wrong reasons, our sins—
yet, remarkably, all the right reasons.
He made us see the real people we are today,
and the real me I am now.

Yesterday,
I remember praying to him for that extra pinch of faith
in myself, just to know that
he is always by my side, no matter what situation
or how I manage to dig myself into a hole.
Jesus pulls me out with holy rays of glory.

Today,
I will face the world with a newer, stronger attitude
conquering all means of failure,
pulling my way to the top without yield.

I am awash in the Holy Spirit that fills our minds
and hearts with hope and satisfaction
that we can make a difference,
in our lives,
and the world around us.
By knowing this, we, too, are kinder, better persons.

From now till death we all shall stay
the individuals we were set out to be,
using the blessed and remarkable gifts created within us.

This is me.
I am.

Holly Streich

God, as you know, I'm not a saint. But, with your help, I'm far from ordinary. I've learned so much from you and every day you gently guide me, teach me . . . and even when I stray from the path, I know you'll be there to set me straight. God, I just hope that your love for everyone can help me remember that, no matter what happens, I will stay calm, not prejudge. When I follow my heart, I find you. Thank you for everything you give me every day. I love you, God, more and more, each day. Amen.

Joanna Begin

Under the Depths

I never want to follow the flow
Until I see who's there,
Until I know where it's going.
And even then I might decide,
I want to swim the other way
And relish in the current,
Pushing against my skin.
I think I'd enjoy the cleansing rain
Because by pushing me back,
It's driving me ahead.
Towards anywhere
but where the flow is
Because I don't want to be caught in the tide
And swept away.
I'd rather walk on the bottom of the ocean,
Sideways, like a crab.

April Kelley

God, thank you! I don't think that I realized how precious my life
is until I realized I had seen a glimpse of heaven. Everything You have
made is part of heaven. My life has never seemed easy to me, yet I
understand now that you have a purpose for *everything*—my actions,
words, and thoughts. It is part of a master plan called "Love."
Even through the bad times, there has been love. It is like my air,
food, sustenance. Without love we are all nothing. Please help me to
live my life by doing Your will, doing Your will to the fullest, by the
best of my ability. Teach me the love, peace, and understanding that
I lack in life. Through my growing, learning, crying, and always I
know that you are there. *Always!* If I forget, all I have to do is look
around. I see you in everything. You are love. Thank you for my
guardian angels for they have been there for me too. *Awesome!*
That is the only word I could think of when I think about everything.
Life, Your son Jesus, family, friends, and every small detail that
makes everything so complete. Thank you! Amen.

Erin Scheel

In a spiraling world,
God is the center point.
Our focus is directed forever
to this middle.
The colors of our hearts
swirl and combine
as they near center—
suddenly we see—
God is reflected into all of us.

Sarah Fineberg-Lombardi

When I need you, you help me.
When I'm lost,
you come find me.
When I talk, you listen to me.
You are my Savior.

You're always there to dry my tears.
You hold me up and
calm my fears.
You guide me with a gentle hand.
You died for me.

Kaitlin Baumgardner

God, give me . . .

God, give me kindness,
even when others do not show kindness.
God, give me understanding,
so I may grow in wisdom and grace.
God, give me hope,
so I may contribute to a peaceful world.
God, give me perseverance,
in the face of adversity.
God, give me charity,
so that I may help those less fortunate than myself.
God, give me strength,
when I struggle.
But most of all, God,
give me faith, so I may share the light
of your love with the world.

Marissa Holloway

Dear God, we thank you for all that you have done for us and all
    that you will do for us.
Once again, we find ourselves here asking for your help and guidance.
God, please help us to help others, no matter who they are or who
    their friends are.

God, help us to comfort them when they need it, even if it
     may be just a hug.
Please also help us to do things we have feared but know we must do.
Help us to jump that extra height, having no fear, for we know
     you are there with us.
Thank you, dear God, for everything. Thank you for everything. Amen.

Kathleen Ghelli

Dear God,
I would like the earth to be quiet of wars
and free from pollution.
The ocean needs to be washed clean
so it can sparkle in the starlight.
I hope someday someone opens the door to the prison
and no one is there.
And I hope everyone will open their hearts.
Thank you.
Amen.

Michelle Barnes

Dear God,
Thank you so much for this day, for yesterday, and for the
     days to come.
Thank you for guiding us each day, in all that we do.
Please help us to do your will.
We ask you to help those who may have lost you, to seek,
     and find you once again.
Please help those who are ill, and those who have lost loved ones,
          and all others who are suffering in the world.
Thank you so much for being present in our everyday lives,
     we are forever grateful.
Thank you for this wonderful gift of life,
          and wonderful companions with which to share it. Amen.

Kristen Van Leuven

2 planting crocuses: easter in october

Hope from despair, life from death, possibility from depression—all of these are significant issues for adolescents. As Kaela Meyers says in her prayer, "When something tragic happens, they pretend that I don't know, pretend that I don't see, pretend that I don't hear—but I do have eyes and I do have ears." Raising issues of grief and hope in the midst of sadness in all its forms near the beginning of the youth ministry year is important. Issues opened very gently now will become discussions in greater depth later in the year. The theological truth of Easter in October mixes the fun of silly bonnets and egg hunts with the possibility of sensitive conversation in a safe context.

YOUTH MINISTRY ACTIVITIES

Issues of loss, grief, hope, and resurrection are handled differently at different ages. Here are several activities that can be used in different combinations depending on the maturity of the group.

Bulbs and Leaves

Spend several hours raking autumn leaves and planting bulbs either at the church or for elderly members of the congregation. After an active and exhausting afternoon return to sit around a low table with a basket of leaves and a basket of bulbs.

Remind the group of the truth displayed seasonally by the death of leaves that promises new budding in the spring and of the need to plant bulbs now in order to have the flowers later. Pass the baskets around and ask each person to choose a dried leaf and identify something in his or her life that needs to be raked up, stripped off. Perhaps it is something beautiful, like a scarlet maple leaf, but it is part of the past. Then pass the bulbs—crocuses or tulips—and ask each one to identify something that is a possibility for the future, something that needs care now to grow and that may not even be apparent for a while. This could be a commitment to good grades, an athletic ability that involves a lot of practice, a mended relationship with a sibling, a romance, or a personality change. Be clear that a possible response during the circle is to hold the bulb silently, rather than sharing out loud. They should take the bulbs home and plant them.

Easter in October

In the Christian tradition every Sunday, not only Easter, is a celebration of the resurrection. The group is going to celebrate the resurrection without being dressed up, and with a small group of people instead of a stuffed-full church. Begin by having the youth group members write out answers to this "Easter Quick Quiz."

1. Do you remember an Easter outfit (or piece of clothing) from younger years?
2. What is your favorite Easter cultural symbol (Easter eggs, butterflies, bunnies, etc.)?
3. What was the first funeral you ever attended (or person or animal whom you were close to who died)? Do you remember your feelings?
4. How much do you remember about the Easter story?
5. What person (a personal friend/relative or a public figure) do you hope is raised from the dead?

Now members of the group find one partner to share the answers to the first question. Allow three or four minutes and then ring a bell. Each person finds another person to share the answers to the second question. Each member will talk with five others. Giving these instructions in the beginning will help them plan partners with whom they are comfortable to share the more sensitive questions.

Next, for fun, divide into small groups with a wide range of "recycle treasure" to prepare an Easter bonnet competition, or dye Easter eggs, or create a butterfly banner, perhaps by gluing autumn leaves in a butterfly shape. Any of these craft ideas will allow the group to share the concept of "Easter in October" with the adult congregation on the following Sunday.

Finally, hold an Easter egg hunt with hollow plastic eggs. Fill them with candy (M&M's and jelly beans are good choices) and little portions of the resurrection story from Luke 24: 1–12—no more than a verse or half a verse in each egg. Eat the candy and save the verses for the worship service.

WORSHIP SERVICE—HALF A COMMUNION

Set a table with a colorful autumn-themed cloth and baskets of leaves, any Easter eggs that have been dyed, bread (maybe bread sticks or pita), and enough balloons for everyone. There is no chalice on the table.

Scripture: Luke 23:33–46, the Crucifixion

Pass out the balloons and have pins available. Go around the circle and have each one break a balloon, after referring to a contemporary tragedy like AIDS or world hunger. Allow a mixture of nearby and distant concerns.

Prayer

God, you are love in the purest sense.
But the fact that love fades and breaks hearts and lives makes me
    wonder if you exist.
Why do bad things happen to people who don't deserve it?
Maybe the problem is that religion is faith and faith is based on trust.
So I can only trust that you are there. Amen. (*Daniel Kamen, p. 20*)

Scripture: Luke 24:1–12

These verses from the Easter story are inside the eggs. Have members read the scripture spontaneously in whatever order emerges.

Prayer

God, when I no longer care for your creation, help remind me how precious it is. When I feel as if the winter or the darkness will never end, show me the dawn or the spring. When I think about death or dying, remind me that life is a gift. And, when I have lost all meaning or purpose, remind me of your awesome plan. As you have saved me, I may save another. As you have taught me, I may someday teach another. As you have loved me, I may love another. Amen. (*Leslie Hoffman, p. 22*)

Scripture: Luke 24:13–35

Don't read it. Invite an acting-out of the scripture with the following instructions to the group:

Two of you stand up (*beckon to two members*) and pretend that you are in the first century. One of you is Cleopas, and you were both followers of Jesus although you were not disciples. There were many men and women who followed him but were not named in the Bible. You are both terribly sad as you leave Jerusalem and head for your hometown of Emmaus. Start walking around the outside of our circle. Imagine how lost and unhappy you feel about Jesus' death.

Somebody joins the two of you. Here (*pointing to another person from the circle*) you take this role and join them. As you walk with them toward Emmaus, ask them why they are so sad. Cleopas is amazed that you don't know about Jesus' death and tells you about it and about how much hope everybody had that Jesus would be the Messiah. Remarkably, even this morning some women went to Jesus' tomb and found it empty and came back and told everybody that they had seen angels and that Jesus was alive. Now you—you are really Jesus, but the other two don't recognize you—comfort them and explain that this is what needed to happen.

Now you have all arrived at the village of Emmaus. Jesus is going to head out, but Cleopas and what shall we call you—Sarah?—convince him that it's dark and dangerous on the road and that he should come in to the house and stay the night. That's very nice of you—after all he is a stranger and these are dangerous times! Well, you have convinced him. You don't have much to eat, but you do have bread. You are going to ask the stranger to say grace and break the bread. Jesus, show us how you would do that.

Suddenly as this stranger breaks the bread, Sarah, you and Cleopas realize that it's Jesus and he is alive. But he vanishes. You two don't even stay to have dinner. Cleopas and Sarah, you may sit down now, but what you really did was run all seven miles back to Jerusalem and tell everybody else that you saw Jesus and recognized him when he broke bread.

Invitation

Easter Communion is half a Communion.
Just as Jesus broke the bread in the house in Emmaus
and then vanished from Cleopas and Sarah's sight,
so we are taught to receive the bread and
sometimes to go into our everyday lives and find the cup.
Communion isn't concluded inside the church walls.
We are going to share this bread and then
somewhere this week you are going to drink the "cup" of faith.
Maybe it will be at your family dinner table,
as you feel particularly close to parents or brother or sister.
You don't need to tell them, but just recognize it yourself.
It may be in the school cafeteria,
when you invite someone to sit with you
who is usually on the outside of social groups,
someone who is often picked on.
Maybe you will have the chance soon to volunteer at a soup kitchen,
or to visit someone in a nursing home,
or to invite a neighborhood kid in to make cookies,
or to do something special with a child you are babysitting,
or to give someone a hand in the checkout line at the grocery store.
These are places God offers you the communion cup, the Easter cup.

Consecrating Prayer

Spirit of God, come upon this bread
that it may be the presence of Jesus alive in our midst.
Help us then to run and share your good news. Amen.
(Pass the bread and share it.)

Benediction—Little Things

So precious are the things we do,
The little things that seem so few—
A smile to a stranger, a thank-you to a friend,
Give hope such strength, it's impossible to bend.
Hope is the key to this mixed-up world,
This place where hate is twisted and swirled,
And keeps feuds going and wars at no end.
This life is a gift and hope helps to mend.
The scars and the pains and the wounds held within.
No matter what happens there's one way to win—
Remember the little things where hope can begin. (*Danielle Mann, p. 23*)

prayers by young people

PLANTING CROCUSES

Easter Sonnet: A Prayer

Tentacles sifting the sand in slow motion stroke
a broken piece of coral not yet stiff
with death, its polyps gray and shriveling.
A sand dollar lifted and breezed by the undertow
waits poised, then settles softly back to rest.

I have seen that sand dollar laid outside
the door of a hotel room on the beach-side
by a sunburned child's flip-flops crusted
with sand. Surely it was picked from the sea
at dawn.
    Later its soft brown skin white-bleached
will hang from a red ribbon on a Christmas tree limb.

O Lord, are you praised when the morning like a kiln
bakes and breaks a beached sand dollar, a bark
which simply hardens, its back slightly arched?

Catherine Clement

Dear God, everyone wants a life smooth like a rock worn from the
sea, but all rocks have their jagged edges. Without them, would we
have any experiences? Would we know what it's like to feel, to do,
even to love? Help those people whose lives are silky smooth, worn
soft by the world. Let them have more jagged edges. Amen.

Sadie Purinton

O God, give me the strength
to deal with my own personal demons.
O God, give me hope
so that I can deal with the demons of others.
O God, give us all the chance to thrive
in the light of your love.
Amen.

Siobhan Allen

God, you are love in the purest sense.
But the fact that love fades and breaks hearts and lives
    makes me wonder if you exist.
Why do bad things happen to people who don't deserve it?
Maybe the problem is that religion is faith, and faith is
    based on trust.
So I can only trust that you are there.

Daniel Kamen

Walking through the darkness, the person is standing in front of two
doors. Opening them reveals the strangeness of life, of the human
body. You have no reason to choose one, and yet you do; you have no
reason to feel safe, and yet you are not afraid. From the threshold of
the room something guides you to the wall—maybe the candle burning or the many statues that sit on top of a table and look back at
your past. You feel the power, the hypnotizing pattern of a song. And
in your mind, you quietly thank the music for . . . just being there.

Meghan Good

I walked in the graveyard today and felt the sunlight beating against my hair and streaming over my shoulder blades. Passing by the familiar stones, covered with questions and yearnings and images of your messengers, I stooped to pick up a broken flower, its blossom not yet wilted, and felt your smile upon me. "You are forgiven," you said. "I am with you."

Jessie Bellantone

Aren't You Glad

Aren't you glad she's in Heaven,
Without Alzheimer's, a great big grin, and huge white wings.
Yesterday she met St. Peter just around seven,
With no wheelchair, of course, she walked like a king.

As she glanced around she knew she'd come a long way,
For she's had a great life and is an angel right away.
St. Peter looked down at her life,
A wonderful grandma, mother, and wife.

He knew in an instant this one's got style,
So he sent her through with a great big smile.
As she went through the gates looking around,
Of course an old friend she soon found.

As they hugged and kissed, he asked how she was,
And her reply was, "Fat and sassy," that's what she'd say,
He took her hand to show her around,
Her parents, brothers, and grandson she found.

So you see she is not sad,
But grateful and relieved that she can remember,
Walking and talking, shouldn't we be glad?
As she looks down at her life, "I'm grateful," she said,
"I died an old lady asleep in my bed."

*(Originally read at Mt. Tabor UCC, St. Louis, Missouri,
at her grandmother's funeral)*

Julie Nollman

Prayer for Depression

God, when I no longer care for your creation, help remind me how precious it is. When I feel as if the winter or the darkness will never end, show me the dawn or the spring. When I think about death or dying, remind me that life is a gift. And, when I have lost all meaning or purpose, remind me of your awesome plan. As you have saved me, I may save another. As you have taught me, I may someday teach another. As you have loved me, I may love another. Amen.

Leslie Hoffman

Dear God, please help everyone everywhere in the world realize that even when things get them down and they feel like they might never feel happy ever again, life can still grow brighter and better. Amen.

Annie Lalish

God, my life is like a pine cone. I can protect myself from some things, but there are others from which I cannot. I fear and then, in the face of my worst fears, I laugh. Amen.

Jaci Kernander

God is like a seed,
For those who do not believe;
I believe that God's love is small—
like a seed.
When a person plants a seed
and starts to believe
it will grow into a beautiful flower—
it does.
When a person starts to believe,
God's love starts growing,
blossoming into a flower
of many bright colors.

And then they all know—
God has loved them all along,
and they only had to believe
in a little seed.

Kelton Meyers

Tough paper surrounds the layers inside me, like the daily biases that cover us all. Inside pushing against the crisp and see-through layers, an odd emergence, birth reversed. Inside, I am sheltered by your love, your peace, the bitterness with which I am concealed. Thank you for that which before I never tried, but trying now, I drown in.

Jessie Bellantone

Little Things

So precious are the things we do,
The little things that seem so few—
A smile to a stranger, a thank-you to a friend,
Give hope such strength, it's impossible to bend.
Hope is the key to this mixed-up world,
This place where hate is twisted and swirled,
And keeps feuds going and wars at no end.
This life is a gift and hope helps to mend
The scars and the pains and the wounds held within.
No matter what happens there's one way to win—
Remember the little things where hope can begin.

Danielle Mann

Dear God, I'm confused. In church we are often told that we do not listen to you or see you, that we are sinful because we do not notice your presence. I listen to you and I am sure I hear you. I look for you and I am pretty sure I see you. I know you are here, because you are

everywhere. I find great comfort and happiness in your love. What I am confused about is that so many people don't feel your presence. I am worried, God. In this bright world I am worried about those who take power with evil intentions. Powerful people (mostly men) take advantage of people (for example in Kosovo). Dear God, help me to understand the reasons and to pray for all people.
Your friend, Becky

Becky Carvin

When something tragic happens—
They pretend that I don't know,
Pretend that I don't see,
Pretend that I don't hear,—
But I do have eyes
And I do have ears.
God created me with these,
So I wouldn't be left behind.
Yet you treat me like I'm deaf;
You treat me like I'm blind.
How can I be so different?
And how are we the same?
God created us as equals
Yet you treat me like I'm lame.
I pray you'll understand;
I pray you'll help me through.
For it's my life that's the tragedy,
And God sent an angel—
You.

Kaela Meyers

God, I can't really believe in you right now,
but everything I ever asked for,
and all my happiness will come
when I get out of here
and I'm able to be with my little sister.
Then I'll feel at home.
Amen.

Heather

3 lighting candles: friends & community

The "Empathy Prayer," in the activity section that follows, is a tool I used in leading prayer-writing workshops and offered to youth group leaders with the invitation that they gather prayers to share in this project. Many of the empathy prayers collected in this chapter have the form "My friend . . ." The flexibility of this exercise allows young people to choose a topic that truly is an issue for a close friend or to remain anonymous while writing about an issue that is personally important. It also allows for empathetic imagination as youth "think themselves" into the concerns of others. November is the month of All Saints' Day and Thanksgiving, both appropriate occasions to reflect on mentors and "saints" of the past and peer support and relationships in the present. One part of the theme draws on the AIDS quilt concept and might be appropriate sometime near World AIDS day, December 1, with more specifically AIDS-related activities.

YOUTH MINISTRY ACTIVITY AND WORSHIP

This is an event that combines activity and worship. It has two parts, one focusing on the past and one on the present.

Saints, Mentors, and Friends, Part 1

Read Hebrews 12:1–2 (and perhaps some selected passages from Hebrews 11 such as 11:8–12 and 11:29–38).

Discuss All Saints' Day traditions. Many people have been saints and mentors in our lives. Some of them are teachers, grandparents, neighbors, coaches, pastors . . . perhaps someone who donated blood or a cornea, perhaps someone who made a speech or sang a song that had particular meaning for us. Each person mentally will identify one person who has been a saint, who has passed on the tradition of faith or an inspiring way of life.

One way to share these names is to place on a beautiful cloth candles in different candleholders—using many colors, sizes, and shapes. All the wicks should be previously burned since they represent people who have been around for a while. Each person chooses one and lights it and tells who his or her saint is and why this person is a saint.

Another possibility is to pass out sheets of white paper and a variety of art materials. Explain the AIDS quilt – that each square celebrates all the different things that were special in a person's life. Different hobbies are represented in different corners and favorite words or phrases appear in embroidery. Have each young person make a "quilt square" for a saint or mentor on the paper and then describe the square when presenting her or his saint.

Lay the pieces out on a colorful backing and tape them together like a large quilt.

Prayer

Gracious God, for all these saints we give you thanks.
They planted seeds in our lives, lit candles on our path
    and hugged, urged, taught, counseled, and guided us.
Some of them are recognizable as saintly, and others are not.
Some are still alive, and others are now dead.

Each one is precious to us.
May they be blessed,
    even as they have been a blessing. Amen.

Saints, Mentors and Friends, Part 2

Read Mark 2:1–12

The point is made in this scripture story that Jesus is impressed by the faith of the four friends who go through so much to bring the paralyzed person into the presence of healing. Friends are the most powerful force in the lives of young adults. Each youth group member has many opportunities to influence friends positively or negatively.

Invite the group to write empathy prayers. Each of the following situations can be written on a thin strip of paper and put in a grab bag, or the young people can look over the whole list and choose one for which they would like to write a prayer. The nature of intercession is that sometimes we pray from needs we know and understand, and sometimes we pray, simply and humbly, for situations with which we have no direct contact—and through the willingness to pray, hearts are opened.

Prayer for a Friend or Empathy Prayer

My friend is drinking or doing drugs.
My friend's first child was just born.
My friend smokes.
My friend was just fired from a job.
My friend was diagnosed with cancer.
My friend moved to a new town.
My friend's mother/father just died.
My friend got married last week.
My friend's spouse/child/parent was just sentenced to prison.
My friend wants me to go with her to get an abortion.
My friend recently lost 100 pounds.
My friend just met his/her birth parents.
My friend just moved away from home/went to college.
My friend just got a driver's license.
My friend comes from Bosnia and is trying to decide
    whether to go home.
My friend was stood up for the senior prom.
My friend was responsible for a traffic accident in which
    there were injuries.

My friend is in love with someone who does not reciprocate.

My friend has just shared with me that he is gay/she is a lesbian
    and is not ready to tell anyone else.

My friend was not accepted to any of the colleges to which
    s/he applied.

My friend is dropping out of college against his/her parents' wish.

My friend is lonely.

My friend's parents are divorcing.

My friend attempted suicide last week.

My friend is successful at everything s/he tries except for pleasing
    his/her parents.

My friend is losing his/her eyesight.

My friend had unwanted sexual advances from a
    teacher/minister/coach.

My friend was arrested for possessing marijuana.

My friend is anorexic.

My friend enlisted in the military.

Ask each participant to write a second prayer so that there is a choice
of prayers to share. Go around the circle reading prayers for these serious issues. Clear instructions at the beginning should remind the group
that they are not praying about particular classmates who can be iden-
tified. Gently reinforce this if anyone tries to "guess" particular names.
Have as many blank slips of paper as there are participants and then ask
them to write down and toss in a basket an issue that is "missing" from
the list. These can be prayed for by category ("We pray for our friends
who *are afraid of taking the SAT's, who were injured in athletic events*,"
etc.), or these topics can be used on another occasion.

Closing Prayer

Gracious God, we know that it is often not easy to help our friends.

Sometimes it feels just like opening up a roof with our bare hands.

Keep us from running away and hiding from serious issues.

Help us to interfere; teach us *not* to mind our own business;
    remind us to be the "designated Christian."

We trust that you will honor our attempts to help one another
    by bringing healing and hope to those for whom we care.

God, it is also very hard to receive help from others.

Help us to relax and let friends really be friends. Amen.

prayers by young people

LIGHTING CANDLES

God, give us courage to grow up responsibly.
God, hear our prayer.
God, give us gratitude for all your teachings.
God, hear our prayer.
God, we give thanks for our families and the lessons they teach us.
God, hear our prayer.
God, we give thanks for our friends; help us to be good friends.
God, hear our prayer.
God, let us make the right decision when we feel pressured.
God, hear our prayer.
God, let us use our creativity and energy to help others.
God, hear our prayer.

Ken Bowles, Clayton Christie, Kristin Huddleston, Lindsay Eastman,
Jason Riendeau, Meredith Powell (Jr./Sr. High Sunday School class,
St. Paul's Church (Episcopal), Lancaster, New Hampshire;
teacher, Anne Jackson)

Dearest God,
I pray for all those who feel that they are less than whole,
     for those who are confused,
     for those who lie inadvertently,
     for those who can't live by kind words,
     and most of all . . .
     for those who don't realize that they
are loved and treasured by you. Amen.

Brittany Copp

God, help me reach out to help people in my school and community find you. I know that many of the students who go to my school question your power. Even some people I know who go to church on a regular basis seem lost. They don't understand that you can go to church and stay busy with church things without really believing in you. I pray that you draw them back to you or help me reach out to them in any way I can. Amen.

Kristen Tronsky

God, we are sometimes as frail as a starfish. We too can be battered by the waves of life, and drained by the rough tides in our journey. Help us to be strong and cling to the grains of sand we call friends.

Katherine Spain

God, thank you for friends. They are wonderful to talk to, to hang out with, and they let you spill your guts. Friends help you get through the long road of life. They remind you that tomorrow will be a better day. Friends help you say "goodbye" to your problems . . . just like you do. If I have a problem, I know that I can give it to you, and I won't have to worry about it any more. You are truly an awesome friend.

Tera Tronsky

There is a time of loneliness that we all feel. It feels like no one is with you to help you with your troubles or stay while you feel sad. And yet, all it takes is a flicker of hope and a friendly face to bring you back to your feet, ready to challenge the roads that cross your life. You can pick yourself up and keep going, triumphing over the interruptions and the dangers.

Kathy Garlo

Dear God, I pray for people who are just getting their driver's licenses. I pray that they will be responsible and drive safely. There are many dangers—sudden storms, icy roads, drunk drivers, etc. I pray for you to keep them safe on all their journeys. Amen.

Elizabeth Waste

Dear God, I pray for my friend who has just shared her deepest secret. Also, God, I pray for myself to keep it to myself and not to betray my dearest friend. I pray for us both, God. I pray for us both. Amen.

Kris Kloetz

My friend was just diagnosed with cancer. God, help him survive his treatments and continue his life. Please give me the strength to put aside my fears and be there for him. And if this is his time to leave us, please show him all the beautiful things in the world that he will miss. Many love him and trust you to take care of him and us. Amen.

Gragen Cook

Prayer for Love

Dear God, give me the patience to accept him as he is. Grant me the strength to hold him up in his time of need. Give me the dedication to see him through the good times and the bad. Give me the honesty to say what needs to be said. Give me the intelligence to know when to just be silent. Give me the courage to follow my heart. And bless our past, present, and future together. Amen.

Leslie Hoffman

God, I know that love can be something that fills a life with happiness, joy, comfort, and security, or it can be torment, sorrow, agony, and an endless tunnel of pain. My friend is in love and the person she's in love with doesn't love her back. I want to pray for both people. My friend needs help getting through the tear in her heart. Help her to face reality and to understand that she is only hurting herself more by wanting to be with him. I know that love isn't something you can forget about, but help her move on. And as for the other person, help him to understand what she is feeling, if possible. Don't let him hurt her any more, because no one deserves to have a broken heart.

Tera Tronsky

His eyes grapple with penitence
words cannot embrace.
As I play the part of not-so-innocent bystander
he erects a wall of comfort stories—
memories of nurture, recollections of hope—
less a cloister of redemption . . .
rather, self-inflicted punishment.
A desperate definitive attempt to cloak me from his pain swells
until his eyes reflect repentance the silence won't express.

Maria I. Tirabassi

Dear God, I pray to you that my very close friend will find another job. Losing a job was very hard on him. I'm going to help him until he finds another one. God, I will be the shoulder he cries on, but can you be the one he prays to and gets guidance from? Thank you, my dear Friend. Amen.

Kelly Pleva

God, please help Max as he moves to a new town. I know how difficult it must be to leave his friends behind. God, help him to find new ones and still stay in touch with the old ones. This is a tough time in his life—please give him strength. Amen.

Kristen Tronsky

Dear God, I know a girl who recently came here from Bosnia. She loves it here, but she misses her family and her own country. Now she's debating whether to go back or not. I don't want her to leave, but I think she would be happier with her own family. Please help her to make the right decision, and help me to live with whatever decision she makes. Amen.

Heather Pleva

For my friend:
I know you are lonely,
but you have to be strong.
I will be with you,
so please hold on.
God will be with you,
and your mother or father
will be with you, too.

Jaci Kernander

Dear God, please keep my friend from getting into trouble. Help him to make new friends easily in the new town. And please make sure he has a nice home and likes it a lot. Amen.

Craig Stevens

Dear God, I am praying for the people who have disabilities. When they cannot do what other children do, they get teased. That always makes a person cry. I pray that one day there may be many more cures for diseases and that new ways will be found so that kids with disabilities can do the same things that other children do. I also pray for children who die, that they may die in peace and be happy with you. In Jesus' name, I pray. Amen.

Betsy Quay

God, you have always been there for me in times when I needed help or guidance. You have given me many gifts of love, kindness, and faith. I know others will get just the same gifts. So keep me and my family and friends safe. But also keep the hungry fed, and get the poor money, and give the insecure people security and faith. Amen.

Matt Loos

Dear God, please take care of a girl I know who's flirting with an older man. She is thirteen and he is thirty-eight. She should tell someone. He is taking advantage of her. Help her and help me to help her. Amen.

Josh Tappan

(My friend has just told me that she is a lesbian but she doesn't want anyone else to know.)

They say that life is a journey,
but the road isn't always straight.
In fact, sometimes it's twisted
by the way that people hate.
Other times it arcs like a rainbow.
Secrets are kept, secrets are told
Let's hope it's never too late.

Sarah Fineberg-Lombardi

Dear God, my friend is bulimic. She's lost way too much weight and I'm afraid. We tried to get her help last year, but she closed us out when we did. Help me to be her friend through this, and to show her I care. I want to be brave for her and to teach her to be brave for herself. She is fragile, handle with care. Amen.

Maria I. Tirabassi

Dear God, please make my friend do the right thing next time. I hope you can help him stop this nasty habit. I know for a fact that one too many Camels can give a person a heart attack. I hope he will soon learn the error of his ways. Thank you, almighty God, for knowing that what a young person, underage, does is still very important. Amen.

Andy Quay, Dan Craven

(My friend's father committed suicide. I try to understand how he felt.)

I don't want to be kept in the dark in my own life.
Life shouldn't be sneaking around under the cover of night,
pretending to be shadows,
figments of an overactive,
hormone-blurred, tear-veiled imagination.

I hate to live the way I do,
immersed in a life-support tank of too vivid imaginings,
afraid to unfurl from my comfortable fetus position,
cowering from life itself.
I'm terrified of things I can't see around or probe into,
yet petrified of anything hidden under a shroud of secrecy.

What is left for me to live then,
if I can't confront that which I know
or bear to see anything I don't?

How can I claim to want the light if I'm the one unscrewing light bulbs
and pulverizing circuit breakers?
I can't blame anyone for the darkness
until I uncover my eyes and discover I've been blind.

Some days I think I've almost made it.
In fact, I'm dazzled by sunbeams dancing purple spots across my eyelids
and moved by the tears and sweat of others on my skin
as they tug me out of my cellar and into my life.

But it is an uphill battle,
as though I'm climbing a slide slippery with rain
in my patent leather Mary Janes,
and I just can't seem to get a grip.

I feel their fingers slip away
as I coast down the wet metal
and land in the muddy bottom,
the voices of my dreams pulling back with the usual twine.

In that dark I am allowed to believe—
I want to believe
in one thing.
I am special.
People see me.
I'm not just a shadow playing in the light.

I buried my hurt deep,
safe behind walls so thick,
the greatest fortress would be put to shame.
Whenever I discovered a gap in my protection
I would run to spare you the pain
I knew you couldn't handle.
Even when you reached out to help,
I realized the extent of your sacrifice.
You would lose your innocence,
everything that was pure and good.

So I acted.
I ran farther than ever before
and jumped

to save you.

Maria I. Tirabassi

4 holying days

Most of the prayers in this section relate to either Thanksgiving or Christmas. There is one each for the holidays of Passover, Veterans Day, and Memorial Day. It would be interesting to engage young people in a discussion about the variety of holidays throughout the year. The particularity of holidays may be lost after elementary school for the young adult and adult population as "a three-day weekend" becomes the definition for many observances which in the past were more distinct.

YOUTH MINISTRY ACTIVITIES

This set of activities is for a December meeting of a Christian youth group. It allows the young people to be engaged in several different groups before a plenary discussion. The depth of sharing in each of these opening exercises will be automatically adjusted by the level of maturity of the participants, but each offers an opportunity for some new understandings.

Christmas Ghosts

Each youth group member should find a partner and share a "Ghost of Christmas Past"—a poignant Christmas memory from a younger age (say under seven). Switching partners, tell about a "Ghost of Christmas Present"—something memorable from last year's Christmas, perhaps, an actual present that was particularly meaningful. Switch partners for the third and last time and share a "Ghost of Christmas Yet to Come"—a particular longing for some emotional/spiritual feeling or occurrence this Advent, something that each one hopes will happen before Christmas Eve.

Christmas—It Boggles the Mind

As an exercise in laughter and prayer, have each young person take one minute to write in a list of single words or short phrases all the images "Christmas" conjures up. They should free-associate—from gift wrap to candy cane—and write as quickly as possible. Then they should divide into groups of four and share the lists, crossing out (as in the game of Boggle) any words that appear on more than one list. The words that are left are each person's "personal" Christmas list. Invite them to write a prayer that includes those words.

Those who are comfortable doing so should share their prayers, or they can be saved for the worship later.

"Twisted" Carols

Individuals, pairs, or triads can write new lyrics about consumerism and the "shopping season" to a familiar Christmas tune. Choices could include "Deck the Halls" (Deck the Malls!), "Away in a Manger," "What Child Is This?," "Jingle Bells," "Joy to the World," "The First Noel," "O Little Town of Bethlehem," "Here We Come A-wassailing," and "Rudolph the Red-Nosed Reindeer."

Sing the songs!!

Holiday Discussion

Begin the conversation with the Advent/Christmas season. Use newsprint to create two lists—one of holiday stresses and one of holiday joys. Young people may want to talk about how family behavior changes, how divorce and remarriage affects traditions, how Christmas in adolescence is different from their childhood experiences of it. Move the conversation away from just Christmas and start to name all the holidays of the year—Valentine's Day, Easter, July 4, Labor Day, Thanksgiving, etc. Which ones are their favorites? Discuss why people have holidays—both the rest-value and the party-value. Then plan a "perfect holiday." Try to have the group create a holiday that incorporates their favorite aspects of all the holidays (fireworks and presents, perhaps) and that attempts to avoid the negative dynamics. Give the holiday a name and try to identify what its spiritual significance would be. Consider whether there are ways to make our real holidays more like the "perfect holiday."

WORSHIP SERVICE—A SERVICE OF CAROLS, PRAYERS, AND CRÈCHE FIGURES

Preparation. Give each young person an index card, a pencil, and a strip of paper with a "nonopening" line from a Christmas carol. Give them fifteen minutes to go wherever they want in the church to sit alone and quietly write prayers that include this line (in the same way that the Christmas Boggle prayers included their personal holiday words). Ask them not to put names on the prayers but to include specific prayer concerns if they wish. Ask for decent handwriting or printing. Here are some possibilities:

"The hopes and fears of all the years are met in thee tonight."
"Life and light to all he brings, ris'n with healing in his wings."
"Traveler, darkness takes its flight; doubt and terror are withdrawn."
"And the mountains in reply echo back their joyous strains."
"Disperse the gloomy clouds of night."
"O tidings of comfort and joy, comfort and joy, O tidings of comfort and joy."
"O rest beside the weary road and hear the angels sing."
"Snow had fallen, snow on snow, snow on snow."
"Gems of the mountains and pearls of the ocean."
"When peace shall over all the earth its ancient splendors fling."
"When halfspent was the night."

Collect the cards and redistribute them so that everyone has someone else's prayer. Then light the Advent wreath, sing "O Come, O Come, Emmanuel," and read the "O" antiphons around the circle. The connection of these ancient traditional prayers with the carol will be obvious and will introduce the prayers that have just been written.

Prayers

For the prayer time sing a Christmas carol, read three of the prayers, then sing another carol and read three more prayers—until all the prayers have been read. Don't try to connect the carols with the lines that are used—just go around the room. If there are prayers from "Christmas—It Boggles the Mind," include them as well.

An interesting twist is writing prayers based on a line from a secular Christmas song—just the opposite of the "twisted" carols from the activity time. The carol lines can be given out either in a grab bag or on a full sheet for choosing.

Scripture—Everybody at the Manger

Pass out small brown paper bags and small white "Christmas Eve candles." Each of the bags should contain a figure from a crèche. Use several sets—large and small, brightly colored and plain. Light the candles and listen to a reading of the Christmas story from Matthew and Luke. As the story is read, each person should bring forward her or his figure from the bag at what feels like an appropriate moment. There should be several Marys and Josephs, as well as many angels, shepherds, and magi. Let the youth group members move the figures around to create a tableau. Save this mixed and beautiful nativity display to share with the full congregation on the following Sunday, if not in the sanctuary, at least on a table in the church hall.

Benediction

Stand in a circle and sing a carol so familiar that no paper is needed, and very slowly pass the candles to the right, so that the circle of light is moving. At the conclusion, blow out the candles and remind everyone to keep the light burning in their lives.

prayers by young people

HOLYING DAYS

Thanksgiving Prayers

O God, this morning I looked across a field and saw a perfect dew-drop on each blade of grass, each shimmering sphere no less than a miracle. I saw the autumn leaves colored in infinite shades of red, yellow, and orange. Such perfection no painter could ever reproduce. I noticed how the grains of earth were agitated by the mere flutter of a sparrow's wings. You control even this. Your creation is awe-inspiring, infinite and beautiful. I thank you for allowing me to be a part of it, today and always. Amen.

Leslie Hoffman

O Holy God,
Thank you for bringing us all together here today. Thank you for this wonderful food and drink. Thank you for the warmth of family and friends, here and far away. Thank you, God, for all that you have done for us. Amen.

Kevin Charles Finefrock

Let us pray.
Thanksgiving is a time for family,
Sharing memories, tears, and laughter,
Missing faraway relatives and those who have died.
Thanksgiving is a time for saying goodbye to autumn,
Leaves have fallen and branches are bare,
The moon has a soft golden glow,
Preparations are being made for winter.
Thanksgiving is a time of generous gifts,
A special turkey feast,

Appreciating friendships,
Love for our family.
Thanksgiving is a time of listening, smelling, and tasting,
But most of all,
Thanksgiving is a time of gratitude for our blessings.
Amen.

Alissa De Trude

Dear God, this Thanksgiving I hope you will help us make good food and have fun with family. I hope everyone is there! Amen.

Taylor Renaud

I am thankful for this opportunity to live abroad for a year, but I am more thankful for the people on both ends of the exchange. Americans are so lucky. So far, I have seen no evidence of shelters or soup kitchens here to provide the less fortunate with means other than the streets for survival. Next to most of the middle- or upper-class homes [in Cianorte, Brazil] with little balconies and swimming pools sit small one-floor houses with peeling paint and damaged roofs. People learn to look away. On Thanksgiving especially, I think about those people, and more about the ones I don't see. I hope they are given the chance to have even half of my happiness. My host family of parents, aunts, uncles, and siblings have all made room for me. I am a friend, cousin, daughter, classmate; the people of Cianorte have welcomed me and I am thankful for such a generous community.

Sarah Fineberg-Lombardi

God, bless this Thanksgiving. We thank you for all you have given us. Know that we appreciate our families and our friends, and all our blessings. Thank you for loving and taking care of us so fully. Amen.

Kate Spain

Look up, and an eternity of ancestors look back.
A breathtaking diadem of time is before me.
My very life is held in essence in the heavens.
An immense sense of peace and belonging washes over me.
A tear reflects all the shimmering dreams above,
And I thank everything for life.

Gabriele Sarah Chase

Dear God, We thank you for the great feast that we get every year at this time. We thank you for our family and our friends. Amen.

Molly H. Goolman

Thanksgiving into Christmas

Thanksgiving is a time of togetherness that is celebrated with family and friends. Thanksgiving is also a time to pray for your loved ones with hope that the upcoming Christmas season is joyous for all. Every Thanksgiving I pray for health and happiness in my family. Last year at this time my mom started showing signs of cancer. I prayed at the table on Thanksgiving Day that she would be all right, even though we had no clue yet what was going on with her. As the weeks progressed, she felt worse and was diagnosed with cancer in early December. With Christmas only weeks away, I prayed each night that she would fight her battle with this terrible illness and win. Christmas morning arrived and she was alive and well. This was probably the best Christmas gift I could have ever received. Now I look back and think about how powerful prayer really is. Prayer can help you with lots of problems in life, even if you only say a few words. My holiday prayer for this year will be for health and happiness for every family around the world. I hope and pray that everyone will have a safe and happy season, and that they will be able to share that time with their loved ones or someone important to them. The person I look forward to sharing my holiday season with is my mom!

Kristen Ardolino

Advent

(For lighting the Advent candles)

Dear God,
A candle is lit for the baby born in shadows.
A candle is lit for the woman who prepared food.
A candle is lit for the person who wrote the story
    of this wondrous event.
A candle will always be alight in the hearts
    of those who remember. Amen.

Elizabeth Dyer

Christmas

Rejoice

Rejoice
Let your heart be encircled in light
Christ has been born.

Cherish
Let your heart embrace each miracle
Love unites with peace.

Glorify
Let your heart dance freely with grace
The angels are singing.

Treasure
Let your heart shine its brilliance
Mary has spoken her prayer to God.

Celebrate
Let your heart shed its fear
The angels are smiling above us.

Triumphant
Let your heart give thanks
Our souls beam with gratitude.

Laura Aldorisio

Dear God, I want this Christmas to be the best Christmas of my life.
I want Christmas for people who cannot celebrate Christmas
and for all my relatives in California.
My friends always exchange gifts
and I hope that other people can do so, too.
Thank you for helping us.
Sincerely

Noi Panyanouvong
P.S. Merry Christmas!

Dear God, I hope you will help me get through Christmas. I hope the
food we make is good and my family and I get good gifts. Amen.

Taylor Renaud

God, please let us feel your presence this time of year, when holidays
can add stress for so many of us. Allow us to let go of that stress and
make peace, that we may enjoy and cherish these precious times.
Help us to understand what truly matters, the spirit of the holidays
and being with our families. Amen.

Kate Spain

God, forgive us when the Christmas story becomes just that: a story.
We read the words but fail to take in their significance. We forget
how scared Mary must have been; young, about to have a baby, far
from home and family, and without the comforts we have today.
We forget how nervous Joseph must have been; unable to find his
wife a place to sleep, an outsider in an unfamiliar city, and about to
become a father. We forget the joy of human life; how out of love
God blessed us with a delicate, new, little baby. God, this Christmas
let us remember what a miracle Jesus' birth was, and what a blessing
you have given. Amen.

Leslie Hoffman

Dear God,
Thank you so much for the holiday season.
The animals surely are thankful, too, from the crocodile to the ox.
We're sorry throughout the excitement we don't remember the
reason
And that we only remember what we take out of a box.
Thank you, Jesus, for sacrificing yourself to take away our sins
And we're sorry we don't think of you at this holy time
As we toss crumpled-up wrapping paper in overcrowded trash bins
And without thinking consume gifts from one hundred dollars to
a dime.
So on this Christmas morning while we eat a Pop-Tart,
We'll give thanks to what you've done, for it is fine.
Thank you for all you've given us throughout time, from the
far-off future back to the very start.
Amen.
By Gregory Kelley, if you please

Gregory Kelley

Dear God,
Let me wake to a peaceful morning.
Let everybody be healthy.
Let this day be another whole and beautiful day.
When Christmas comes,
let everyone live in peace.
Amen.

C. J. Bartlett (Chelsea)

P.S. Let everybody receive what they want!
Amen!

Heavenly Father,
Please help us to find our way through this Christmas season.
Help us to see past the presents and instead
Help us to see what we are really celebrating,
The birth of your Son, our Savior, Jesus Christ.
Amen

Jaci Kernander

Gracious God,
Watch over us during this busy season while we are gathering with family, renewing friendships, singing Christmas carols, and listening to sleigh bells jingling. With the smells of sugar cookies and evergreen trees filling the air, do not let our hearts and minds stray from the real meaning of Christmas – the birth of Jesus and the starry night in Bethlehem. Amen.

Alissa DeTrude

Dear God, We thank you for all the presents and family and friends whom we see at this time but do not usually see. Amen.

Molly H. Goolman

Dear God,
Bless all of my friends and family.
Please forgive my sins.
Let this Christmas be wonderful.
My family and I look forward to a great time with cousins.
In Jesus' name I pray.

Tim Panyanouvong

Dear God, in my hand is the evergreen, which stands for many things. For some it symbolizes Christmas, a favorite holiday. But it is also a living thing and other living things live in it and from it. And yet, we cut it and put it in our homes and no one forgets the clean fresh smell that fills our homes with a little forest during the long cold winter. Amen.

Marcy Lombard

Lord, help me remember the promise,
the story we hold so dear.
The baby was born in Bethlehem,
to lie in a manger mere.

The magi came bearing gifts,
And angels began to sing.
I celebrate your day of birth;
And it's myself I bring.

Gabriele Sarah Chase

O Holy God,
You sent your only son to save us on this day. He saved your people
just like you wanted him to. We celebrate this day in his name. Thank
you for the kindness and caring of family near and far. Please help all
those who are less fortunate than us here today, like Jesus would have
wanted years ago. Amen.

Kevin Charles Finefrock

Passover

(Elizabeth's sister is away for a year studying in Brazil. See also chapter 10.)

Getting ready for Passover later this year will be hard. Every year
Sarah and I bicker over who gets to set the table, and who will have
to iron the napkins. This year will be different, no bickering. I will set
the table for all of our guests, and iron all the napkins. It won't be
the same though. I'll set the table for one less person than there
should be. I won't hear her beautiful voice singing the prayers,
won't hear her laugh, and I won't be able to look over and see her
dazzling smile that lights up any room.

Elizabeth Fineberg-Lombardi

Veterans Day

God, when I see a flag I think of the men and women who have
passed on before me and yet left so much. I remember my grand-
father Cornell who was in the World War. I think even further back
of ancestors who were bodyguards for Washington. I think of
religious ancestors like Pilgrims who sought freedom of religion.
I thank you, God, for all they did and the opportunities they gave
me to pass these values on to others. Amen.

Shannon Keeney

A Memorial to Memorial Day

I walk past the iridescent wall,
stretching forever
in remembrance of the dead,
just one more stop on a Greyhound tour.
The little American flags seem to mock me,
and my stone-carved heart.

Yesterday we celebrated them as heroes,
regardless of the scorn previously lashed out.
In the midst of our parades and barbecues
we conveniently forget to tell the little ones
about our abuses.
How the soldiers returned from Vietnam
embittered and impoverished.
When they came for help,
peace banners were shoved in their faces,
and the boys who carried other boys
miles through the jungle
were snidely dismissed,
erased.

It wasn't our war.
It's never our war.
It can't go on.
We have to grow up,
and face every memorial we've built
and keep on building
until even the sentimentals
realize that it isn't enough
just to remember.
It isn't enough
to build even beautiful walls.
What we must do
is learn to celebrate life,
instead of death.

Maria I. Tirabassi

5 new yearing

The New Year's holiday and Epiphany are symbolized liturgically by dreams, stars, opportunities. January is a "second beginning" in the program year that opened in September. The calendar provides an opportunity for revival and breath-catching. For young people, January is a literal beginning of the second semester in school. Prayers gathered in this section focus on dreams—like the magi's; the human need for guidance—like a star; and new beginnings and resolutions—like Jesus' baptism in the Jordan.

YOUTH MINISTRY ACTIVITY

Preparation. In December, divide the youth group into triads and give each group a disposable camera and the assignment to take twenty-seven pictures that illustrate "two-faced January" (named for the Roman figure who looked back to the past year and forward to the next year). Some groups of three simply may pass the camera around so that each person takes nine exposures, while others may discuss their photographs and then go on a "shoot" together.

Pictures should be developed before the meeting, and each group should spend the opening half-hour creating a poster and presentation for their photography. Make poster board, rubber cement, markers, and various other art supplies available. Also have newspapers and magazines available so that each group can use headlines, text, or photographs to further develop their portrayal of this "between-times" point of the year. Adding this dimension of mixed-media collage is a way to include any members who are new, forgot to take photographs, or were not present at the December meeting. Combining newspaper and magazine headlines and photographs with more intimate pictures demonstrates the interface of the personal and the global.

Spectrum on a String

An opening icebreaker or game later in the session will provide the "new beginning" of getting to know members of the group. Stretch a rope or a string down the longest dimension of the room and identify one end as *never, never* and the other end as *always, always*. Tape the ends to walls. Call out these statements of hobbies and habits and have the group move back and forth along the string in response to each statement.

I am an early riser.
I have a favorite TV show I like to keep up with every week/every day.
I play music—tape, radio, CD, instrument—at least once a day.
I love sports.
In order to be happy, once a day I need chocolate.
I need solitude and I don't get enough of it.
I need company (quality friendship) and I don't get enough of it.
I wish I could change my hair.
I have clean closets.
I keep a journal or diary.

I love e-mail and the Internet.
I have a pet who is very important to me.
I have a favorite chair in my house.
I made a resolution on January 1.
I love to cook.
I take a long walk at least once every couple of weeks.
I am completely happy with how my body looks.
I have a sibling I would like to send out on permanent loan.
I love science fiction.
I go to the movies every week.

Close the game with comments on how each person is on the string at different points. No two people have exactly the same coordinates and yet it is one spectrum. There's nothing "completely" different about people.

WORSHIP SERVICE —
REMEMBRANCE OF JESUS' BAPTISM

At this time of year churches often offer a service of renewal of baptismal vows. This is an opportunity to honor water as sacramental in our lives and remember Jesus' baptism as a time of recommitment.

Gathering Outdoors

Worship begins outdoors with an honoring of water. There are two possibilities, one for colder climates and one for warmer ones.

In colder places: Make a snow sculpture together. Enjoy the snow, mold it, play in it, even toss a few lighthearted snowballs. If time is short, make snow "angels."

Come inside and give everyone a piece of paper and scissors. Commenting that every snowflake is unique, have each person cut a paper snowflake and then—fragile as the snowflake form is—each person will write a prayer on his or her snowflake.

In warmer places: Plant something together—individual small potted plants or flowers, a bulb, or a bush for the church. Each person should have a turn watering the plant. Come inside and distribute a pile of leaves. Let each person carefully write a prayer with a magic marker on a leaf.

Cover the worship table with blue cloths, and center a flat bowl of water. Float candles in the water, and arrange as many shells as there are participants around the bowl. Where shells are not easily available, use water-rounded pebbles or lake-glass.

Invocation

Pray the prayers that were written on the snowflakes or the leaves.

Water Stories

Identify the human relationship with water (we *are* water, we drink it, wash in it, cook with it, play in it, swim, ice-skate, ski, walk in the rain or by the ocean, by lakes, or waterfalls). Elicit as many responses as possible. Then ask if anyone has a water story to share.

Thanksgiving Litany for Water

(Give out these lines. Have any three lines read between each unison response.)
We give you thanks, O God, for water.
Over a watery chaos your Spirit moved in the beginning of creation.
Between a flood and a beautiful rainbow you saved people in the time
of Noah.
Through the Red Sea waves you rescued your children from slavery.
We give you thanks, O God, for water.
Jesus walked on water to save his friends from drowning.
Jesus offered living water to a woman by a Samaritan well.
In a basin of water, Jesus washed his disciples' feet,
showing them how to serve one another.
We give you thanks, O God, for water.
In water the disciples were commissioned to baptize all people.
In water people of our tradition are baptized, claiming faith
as their own.
In water parents and godparents bless children.
We give you thanks, O God, for water.

Scripture: Matthew 3:13–17

This is the time of the year when we remember that Jesus began his ministry by making a commitment. He startled his cousin John by being baptized just like everyone else, receiving God's blessing by the Jordan River. January is an important time to make commitments and promises. Please take a shell (or pebble) and put your finger in it. Silently make a promise for this year and press the mental promise into the shell (or pebble) with your finger. Place your shell (or pebble) in the water, immersing your hand. As you lift it out let the hand dry naturally in the air. Feel wet.

Prayer

God, pour your Holy Spirit upon this water filled with our promises.
Splash us with your amazing grace.
Wet us with healing.
Wash us for truth.
Soak into our souls that we may live in faith,
hope for the resurrection,
and drench others with your powerful love.
Rain your blessing on all who seek you—
those who are here with us today,
and all others near and far
who call upon your holy name. Amen.

prayers by young people

NEW YEARING

Thank you, God, for our new beginnings. The shining sun makes me smile at the morning and the birdsong brings me joy. Thank you for the stories you give us from your life that give me the strength to continue living my own life and expecting happiness. Amen.

Gragen Cook

I was a fallen star,
My own light fading.
My hope to be untrue,
My wishes were broken,
My dreams turned to nightmares.

My strength was weakened by my sadness.

The moon lost his faith in me,
The stars had turned away from me;
The darkness filling me,
The gleam in my heart had lost its love.
My whole universe—empty.

But then, suddenly, the Sun,
Her extravagant light,
Her rays reaching out with love,
Her gentle breaks through the clouds shouted with compassion,
Her love shined to my heart's center,
Her brilliant faith in me touched my soul.

My love returned,
My faith restored,
My strength overcome,
My luminous soul lightened until the darkness slowly disappeared.

I am a shooting star,
Circling over God's majestic kingdom,
Reaching out my peace to others,
Glittering the heavens of the sky.

Laura Aldorisio

Dear God, I am a teenager that always causes trouble, but I won't now, if you help me. I want to get out of placement and home to my family and my school, so that I can make something of myself. I don't want to be a troublemaker. I will try to read the Bible every night so that I can believe in God and Jesus and have faith in myself. Thank you for taking your time and listening to me. I will try to stay off drugs when I get out of here. I'm going to have a normal life. Thank you, God. Amen.

Mike Gavard

Dear God, thank you for filling our empty rooms and dark places with light. We remember your everlasting love, when we open our hearts and minds for you to fill with your Spirit. Amen.

Meaghan Maguire

Meaghan Maguire

Light a candle
Write your dreams
Circle around the food of your imagination.
Wood, wicks, wheat
All variables in a world
of so many differences.

Elizabeth Dyer

Dear God,
We are approaching the new millennium. We are scared and we are worried. Are you coming with it, God?

What signs will we see? Protect us from false prophets, earthquakes, famine, and war that some of us are expecting. Help us not to be deceived. People's love will grow cold. Evil will spread. We need you, God. How can we face the future? We are confused.

Help us to stay faithful and remain Your servants. We want to be prepared for You every day. We want to serve You. We will praise You using our gifts and talents. Keep us close to You.

We wonder if we are living up to your expectations, God. Do we live the Way, the Truth, the Life? Help us. Teach us. Don't leave us on our own.

We love You very much and we want to please you, God.
We want to be ready for our future with faith. Amen.

Teen Class, Faith United Church of Christ, Hazelton, Pennsylvania

Dear God, please keep my family and friends safe during the coming year 2000 and especially from Y2K problems. Please keep computers all over the world going and strong. Please keep my family safe and happy on trips and help my brothers and sisters to be safe skiing and snowboarding. Thank you for keeping us in your care. Amen.

Nathan Guelli

Dear God, will you help me through these rough spots in my life. I am a fourteen-year-old girl and I am trying my hardest to change the wrong things in my life that got me where I am. I'm asking for help. I'm asking for guidance. I'm asking you to lead me on the right path—and that would be the path home. Amen.

Natalie

God, you are my path to freedom.
You protect me from evils.
You, Lord Jesus, are my Father—you were the only one who cared.
I know that you will give me life in the garden of faith.
I need your help and I will do my best to accept it.
Please let this prayer live in my heart
and in the hearts
of those who will read it.
Amen.

John Dionne

Dear Lord, would you please
let my spirit soar as an eagle.

In the days of forsakenness,
when money clouds judgment,
please guide me in your wisdom
to become fruitful.

Please help me discover your kindness and truth,
the power You have. Amen.

Anonymous, Storrs, Connecticut #1

Dear God, the smoke was so thick it was hard to see. The rocket began racing toward the sky. Although it was just a model, not even an eighth of the size, I dreamed it was the space shuttle Apollo. I dreamed it was racing to the moon, about to make history. I prayed for their safe journey, to and from this barren place, hoping the information to be gathered would help the world, God's world, in some way. My small rocket landed on the ground and I imagined how happy the astronauts would be when they returned, and how I wish that I could be there. This is my dream, God. Someday . . . Amen.

Kris Kloetz

Dear God, I pray that I don't kill myself snowboarding. I don't mind injuries as long as I can snowboard after they heal. In fact, if you can keep me safe as a young boarder, when I'm an adult I'll take responsibility to be safe and not fall to my death. (Also please let me raise the cost of a Joyride snowboard.) Snowboarding is what I love, God. Amen.

Anonymous, Lancaster, New Hampshire

Beauty Tips from Experts

Physical beauty is like lard. It makes food taste
good, but what the hell can a lump of lard do on its
own? Honest beauty is where it's always been
(under those layers of skin and makeup and Oil of
Olay to fight the wrinkles—are you sure you aren't
ugly?)
So your complexion is peaches and cream. Maybe
it's time to exfoliate your soul. Scrub your dead and
dull outer shell away. So your lips have been called
supple. I think that now is the time to replenish your
heart. Maybe a blemish wouldn't dare risk
the purity of your skin. Take a moment and cleanse
your mind. So maybe you're what they call
beautiful. But I'll have to look again because at first
glance you were invisible.

April Kelley

You Give Me Strength

You give me strength
To write and write,
Till there be no light
To write at length.

Whether I be morose
Or up and sound,
As long as you're around
I shall write my most.

If my pen doth freeze
I merely think on thee,
And you speak to me
As the cool breeze.

You're my inspiration,
My reason to write.
My dear, your sight,
Bringeth temptation.

Adam Kernander

Prayer

When we are confused, you help us understand.
When we are lost,
you help us find our way.
When we are sick or sad,
you answer our prayers.
When we feel like we have nowhere to turn,
you are there.

We thank you, God, for your love.
We thank you for your compassion and patience.
We thank you for delivering us from evil.
You always stay on our side.
through the happy times,
the sad ones,
and even the intolerable ones.
Without you we would be lost and
the world would be dark,
but you are there
and we thank you.

Nicole Messmer

Our dear God, You spend your time creating creatures so mighty and so hard to hide and human beings to spread your word. Your teachings come straight from the heart of wisdom. O God, let us hold ourselves back for this wonderful ride we call life. Now we know we can make it through and we praise you and thank you. Amen.

Bethany Elliott

Dear God, Happy Birthday to me.
I am now a year older.
Help me to make better choices than last year.
Keep me safe
to live a long and happy life.
Amen.

Elizabeth Burns

6 reaching out

Social justice issues for young people are as near as the school cafeteria and as distant as news stories on CNN. The prayers in this chapter reflect both of these dimensions. The youth activities focus on more local concerns. They are adapted from a youth ministry piece I wrote to accompany Bryan Sirchio's song "The Table of Friendship and Love," found on his CD *The Artist's Hand.* The worship service moves into the global arena (literally!). By this time in the year, there is probably enough trust and mutual respect for long periods of meditation in worship, but some groups may find this difficult and the times for reflection can be shortened.

YOUTH MINISTRY ACTIVITY

Gather in a circle of chairs around a low table with a large candle or hurricane lamp and a large salt shaker in the center. Prepare by cutting multicolored 8½" x 1½" strips of construction paper (eight to a standard 8½" x 11" sheet).

Read Matthew 5:13–16

Remind the group that, on the simplest level, this scripture from what we call the Sermon on the Mount suggests that we live out our Christian faith in one or both of two ways. We are the "light" (*light the candle or hurricane lamp*) when we do very visible things—when we participate in church, youth group, or mission activities. At other times we can be "Christian salt." Salt disappears when it is in food—it is tasted but not seen. School is one of the places where Christian behavior is felt and experienced by others in spite of the fact that we don't walk around continuously identifying ourselves as "Christian."

Links of Love

Pass out eight strips of colored paper to each participant and have them write on each one the designation of a different group from their school. This is a purposely large number so that they mentally stretch to include "groups" they might not otherwise have thought of as distinct identities. In addition to nerds, populars, rappers, honor roll kids, athletes, and new kids in town, open-ended questions might draw out some other suggestions—"born agains," gay and lesbian students, members of the swim team, kids with English as a second language, left-handers, students with disabilities, virgins, Jewish students, trailer park or project kids (or some other neighborhood designation). Strive for variety so that everyone present is in one or two groups. Have the participants throw their strips into a basket and draw out eight other ones to read. Continually turn the conversation away from criticizing particular groups and back to the emotional impact of being on the inside of some groups and the outside of other groups. Collect the strips again and have two volunteers turn them into a chain of paper loops while the second activity is taking place.

Duck, Duck, Salt

Based on the childhood game "Duck, Duck, Goose," this game suggests that people try to duck out of personal responsibility to welcome people. A volunteer who is "it," or the leader, begins by naming *one* thing he or she could do to include an outsider. That person then walks around the circle with the salt shaker saying, "Duck, duck, duck," and then sprinkles someone's shoulder or head, shouting, "Salt!" and that person must come up with one suggestion to bring an outsider in. Continue to play until everyone has had a turn and everyone is pretty salty.

WORSHIP SERVICE

This service has time for personal reflection. In some groups that may be done in silence, but also it would be appropriate to use popular music in a sacred context. A small group could discuss and plan music for these times and then work the CD player. Some suggestions might be Jewel's "Hands," Jann Arden's "If God Were One of Us," Sarah McLachlan's "Angel" or "Do You Remember Me?"

Preparation. Provide a large stack of newspapers. Have members of the group look through them and clip headlines of "contemporary crucifixions"—places in the community, nation, and world where there is "bad news."

Come together around a table on which are a tall cross, a globe, a basket of Band-Aids (out of the wrappers), and tape. Each person will read a headline he or she has cut out, tape it to the cross, and then wind it around as the group responds:

"The cross is wrapped in the news of our days."

Continue until all the headlines have been twisted around the cross. At the end the leader will say:

"Let us reflect on how Christ, the crucified One,
  can make a difference in contemporary crucifixions."

Give ten minutes of silence or musical interlude.

Scripture: Revelation 21:3–4 and 22:1–2

Pass out the unwrapped Band-Aids. Pass the globe around and have each person place a Band Aid on the globe and name an "intercession"—a region of the world's community that needs healing or blessing. Welcome a mixture of personal concerns with the global concerns if they arise.

Members of the group may wish to share their thoughts and ideas. Some specific ideas for mission activities or advocacy in social justice concerns may be offered. Other groups may prefer to wait for discussion until another time.

At the end the leader will say:

"*Let us reflect on the tears of the world, the healing needs*
      of the nations,
   and how we can bandage them with the leaves of love."

Give ten minutes of silence or musical interlude. In closing, put the salt shaker and the candle or hurricane lamp back on the table so that the four objects (salt shaker, candle, cross with headlines, globe with Band-Aids) form a cross.

Prayer

Gracious God, we come humbly
before the pain of your cross
and the tears of the world.
Season us with the salt of your Spirit
and light a candle of faith,
of courage, of justice,
and of hope,
in each one of us,
through Jesus Christ our Savior. Amen.

prayers by young people

REACHING OUT

Prayer in the Red Dust

Prayer in the red dust
for the children who live here
the thin brown-eyed future of Mazatlán
who are ever betrayed by money

Prayer in the red dust
for the coughing baby
held and rocked by sister
like a life-sized doll
as the pastor makes a passing comment
about respiratory illness

Prayer in the red dust
for all those who surround us
the silent, work-worn ring
that says nothing
as their children snap photos
of gringos and children
playing games and spinning

Prayer in the red dust
for those who aren't just tourists
and never have the option
of buying comfort with a Visa Gold

Prayer in the red dust
for those who think
that we are always right
and only America
can fix the world
those who can turn a
blind eye to what we support
gold coasts, guns, street kids,
the bomb bully of the block

Prayer in the red dust
for this happy and sad world
this sweet and sour
bittersweet sharing
of prayers in the cloying red dust

*(Written after a mission trip to Mazatlán, Mexico, by a member of
First Congregational Church, UCC, Corvallis, Oregon)*

Mary Beth Budd

The candle of hope burns alone. Out of its brightness comes a vast
brilliance of love. This is the way it happens—one candle lights another,
then the lights keep flickering on as the confidence grows. Sometimes all
it takes is a voice, and out of that voice comes the song of a million.

Kathy Garlo

This is a prayer for everyone, anyone, but especially all the someones who have never had a prayer said for them. We are different from one another—sometimes we are strangers to one another. No two journeys ever follow exactly the same path. But all of us have our troubles and worries. All of us need reassurance as we stumble along the roads we choose to take; and that assurance must come from the one we can truly put our trust in, the only one who could really understand all the different choices, hardships, joys, and feelings that have combined to make us the individuals that we have each become. Hallelujah, amen.

Alexandria Smith

I pray
that all the storms are changed
to peace,
all the bullets
are changed to chocolate,
all the prisons
are changed to gardens,
and all the defeats are changed
to touchdowns.
Amen.

Nathaniel Ash-Morgan

Where Has It All Gone?

They ask us, "Where have all the flowers gone?"
And I want to add:
"And where has all the laughter gone,
and where have all the giggles gone,
and where has all the innocence gone,
and where has all the happiness gone,
and where has all the hope gone,
and where has all the truth gone,
and where has all the peace gone,
and where has all the beauty gone,
and where have all the children gone?"

And I am answered,
"They've been shushed and stifled,
and the innocence was lost,
happiness was voted down last month
and all hope went out of fashion.
The truth was decided to be unjust,
and there was nothing in the budget for peace.
Beauty seems to be misplaced,
And as for the children, it was decided there was no more time for
that."

April Kelley

What We're Missing

Time goes by minute by hour.
Caring and loving? We don't have time for such!
As we always try to gain more power,
We forget the things that mean to us so much.

Tyler Martin

Though we are all different,
we share many things in common.
Each of us is a piece of the puzzle.
Without the other pieces,
the picture is incomplete.

Justin Koonz

God, you make the music come. When people get mad, they calm
down. When they are sad, they become happy. God, you are like a
flute and you make music through all the people who have talent with
flutes and other instruments. God, you make the music come. Amen.

Erica White

Dear God, thank you for making such a beautiful world for all the plants and animals. You have blessed us with such a bright glowing sun, cool refreshing rain, vibrant rainbows, and green-leafed plants. Forgive me for all the sins I have committed today and at other times in my life. Forgive others, even the ones I do not want to forgive—like Adolf Hitler, Saddam Hussein, Fidel Castro, Slobodan Milosevic. Forgive even those who kill mosquitoes in frustration. Please watch over everyone on the earth—especially all of the animals. Let fighting cease. May people love; may they rejoice and hug; may people care not only for their families but also for strangers they meet. Love and caritas.

Kaitlin Baumgardner

I pray to dream
about lilies and stars.

I'd love not to dream of hate.

I pray to live
in a lavender field
with no sadness, jealousy, or silence.

Anonymous #2, Storrs, Connecticut

Dear God, sometimes I think my life is as hard as a rock.
Some decisions I make are so hard to decide. Amen.

Jeremy Mann

God, even though the orange is sometimes bumpy and uneven on the surface, the inside is always sweet when the skin is peeled. This is like people—all good and equal inside, no matter how they show it on the outside. Amen.

Tyler Martin

Dear God, I pray to you to help those people who have no home. Owning a home can be expensive. I wish they were less expensive, and that everyone could have them. Everybody has problems, but it's easier to deal with them if you can go home at night. I am not sure what you can do, but I know I always want to give a part of my prayers to homeless people. In Jesus' name, I pray. Amen.

Katherine Christopher

Dear Lord Jesus, please help all the less fortunate people. Please help the people who do not know about you and your ways. Please help them learn to do the right thing—to do what you would do in that situation. Amen.

Anonymous, Lancaster, New Hampshire

God, help us to understand and know the one that wears a working glove. These hands are spent in labor and in toil done out of love and care. There is good that comes from all people. There is satisfaction in the value of earning a living. We all create, work, try, in our different ways, but each one of us is still forever learning. Amen.

Meghan Good

Dear God,
Please let there be world peace.
Let the world end fighting.
Let the people cease to hate.
Let us all be of equal power under you.
Let us learn to respect one another.
Take us into your healing hands, so we may all love one another.
Let there be hope for a new beginning, with enough food and
    shelter for all.
Accept us all into your realm of heaven.
    In Jesus' name we pray. Amen.

PHISH (Pilgrim Helpers in South Hadley), First Congregational Church,
South Hadley, Massachusetts, Youth Group—
Ken Bozek, Reghan Garton, Sarah Lovelace, Cory Rundle

(Written during the conflict in Kosovo)
Dear God, can you please tell us why?
Why is it that all these people must die? The war is swirling around
us, yet we close our eyes. Bomb here, bomb there—another one dies.
We would like to go back to that place we call home. The thought of
all these people dying hurts me inside. I want to go to help them. The
human race is so wrong. Help us, O God. We all want to go to that
place we call home. Amen.

Bethany Elliott

My loving God,
Please help all of the people in this world get over their differences
and just get along with each other. Protect us from the evil in this
world. Please keep us healthy and help us to make the right choices.
Help all of the families who have lost loved ones due to violence.
Forgive those who have made the wrong decisions. And most of all,
please forgive us all for our many sins.
Always ♥,

Allen M. Burbey, Jessica Jung, and two friends

Hey God,

It's me again. I love the feeling of knowing that, if anything's ever troubling me, I can come to you. Who would be better to talk to than the Almighty for comfort and wisdom?

The reason I'm calling on you? Columbine! I know we have discussed this just after the tragedy happened. You showed me how deep darkness and evil can run and how broken people do broken things. You also helped me understand how deep hatred for one human being from another can be. People who refuse to acknowledge your everlasting love, peace, and wisdom are leading physically and spiritually broken lives.

As time goes on I can feel the roller-coaster ride that the survivors and their families are riding. I know that many of those families know you. I know that you are with them and carrying them. My prayers are not only for those families but also for those who are not able to turn this over to you. Not able to turn this tragedy to your honor and glory. I know that on their own they cannot forgive, but it must be done through you.

What will happen to those? What type of life physically and spiritually are they cultivating for themselves? Because of the decisions that they choose to make in bitterness and hatred are they going to recreate the tragedy again?

I hear you, Lord. Your light and love for your people in Columbine will stand strong. They, along with all of us who have received the burden, must continue to pray for the others. Amen.

Dawn Snyder

With a gun to her head, she still said yes.
Yes, she believed in God.
He pulled the trigger.
He ended her life because of her beliefs.
The next one had no choice.
He died because the boy with the gun
said he hated black people.

He was different, so he was dead.
He didn't even have the option to say something to save
himself.
"Jocks stand up, we're gonna kill you all."
Of course, the jocks didn't stand.
Still those boys wanted to kill them,
all because of their hobbies, their clique.
I would not have died.
I am white, I am not a jock,
I do not even believe in God.
I would still be alive.
But maybe I wouldn't.
Some kids died. Just because.
Wrong place, wrong time.
Helping other people escape from death.
I would have helped them.
Definitely.
I wish all that hate would go away.
So much hate in the world.
Hate that caused the shooting rampage.
I cry.
For the kids at Columbine.
Because of fascism.
Rape, murder, brutality.
Ignorance.
The people who died could not do anything about it.
How could those boys hate something so much,
that they could kill.
Or maybe they didn't hate.

Mari Tyndall-Lambe

Dear God, please give me the courage to face each day with a positive
outlook. Help me to overcome the violence and disrespect displayed
by many teens today. Give me the strength to deny any urge to participate in the violence and injustice that takes place. Guide me through
each day with your love and forgiveness. Amen.

Kristen Lisak and a friend

7 healing and hoping

Young people have as many questions about the issues of healing as everyone else who sits in the pews of faith communities. Why are people ill? Why do accidents happen? What is the impact of prayer on physical situations? Is there a difference between healing and cure? Do we believe in miracles? Do we believe in medicine? How do we respond to people who are ill or people who are grieving? Are sad situations a part of a divine plan or is it the case that God gives people an opportunity to bring some good out of a tragic occasion for which God is not responsible? The prayers in this section show that there are no simple answers and that holding the question open is often very important. Prayers on these issues can be found in other chapters, including a number of prayers for friends in chapter 3 and Kristen Ardolino's prayer about her mother's cancer in chapter 4.

YOUTH MINISTRY ACTIVITY

Divide the group into small groups of at least four members. Each group will have a situation about which it imagines the details. One person will role-play receiving a visit from the others. Each visitor will present a different perspective on the situation. The instructions should be clear that the "actors" do not convey their own personal opinions during the skit but rather state extreme positions. After the skit, the whole group can discuss the issues raised.

Story—Traffic Accident

There has been a traffic accident. The group decides what happened. One person is in the hospital. The group decides whether this was the driver and how serious the injury is. Three friends go to visit. What do they say?

Story—Addiction

A high school student has an addiction. The group decides what this is after discussing all the possibilities. This person has a school or family crisis today because of the addiction. The group decides what it is. Three friends meet the fourth one "accidentally on purpose" standing by the school lockers. What do they say?

Story—Grieving

A middle-school student's mother or father has died. The group decides the cause. Three friends are going to visiting hours at a funeral home. What do they say?

Story—Disability

A young person has moved into town and into the church community. This person has a disability. The group decides what it is. (Consider limitations on mobility, vision or hearing, and mental retardation in creating this situation.) Three members of the church youth group are going to visit this newcomer. What do they say? (*Remember to present different perspectives here. One or two of the "actors" can be tactless.*)

Story—Cancer

A middle-school student has cancer. The group can decide what kind of cancer, how life-threatening it is, and what treatment has taken place (for example, whether there has been hair loss). Three friends visit in the hospital. What do they say?

Story—Unexpected Pregnancy

A high school girl is pregnant. The group can decide whether the young man knows, and how exactly this situation is complicating the girl's life, as well as how far along in the pregnancy she is. She calls her three best friends and asks them to come over to give her "advice." What do they say?

All of these situations elicit complicated responses. Each one, as written, asks for verbal input. A concluding audience question would be not just "What did they say?" but "How did they listen?" Allow the discussion to take its own course. Help participants withdraw from right/wrong judgment. Finally, read together and discuss the real-life situation posed by Rebecca Ann Duger's reflection and prayer at the end of this chapter.

WORSHIP SERVICE

This is a healing service—a time when we pray for physical, emotional, and spiritual healing and hope for ourselves, for those who are dear to us, and even for those we may not know.

(*Preparation*) Place five coats around the room. Possibilities include an athletic "letter" jacket, a homeless person's ragged coat, a grandmother's shawl, the "littlest angel" costume from the Christmas pageant, and a long leather trench coat or other popular style of coat. If there is a worship bulletin with scriptures and intercessions printed, attach a small piece of fabric to each bulletin with a paper clip.

Scriptures for Healing

(*Each of these scriptures may be read by a different young person.*)
Heal me, O Lord, and I shall be healed; save me and I shall be saved; for you are my praise. (Jeremiah 17:14)

But for you who revere my name the sun of righteousness will rise, with healing in its wings. (Malachi 4:2)

When Jesus saw her, he said, "Woman, you are set free from your ailment." When he laid his hands on her, she stood up straight and began praising God. (Luke 13:12–13)

. . . to another faith by the same Spirit, to another gifts of healing by the one Spirit. (1 Corinthians 12:9)

He himself bore our sins in his body on the cross, so that, free from sins, we might live for righteousness; by his wounds you have been healed. (1 Peter 2:24)

On either side of the river is the tree of life with its twelve kinds of fruit; and the leaves of the tree are for the healing of the nations. (Revelation 22:2b)

Prayer

Spirit of the living God,
elusive as the wind, gentle as the dove,
cleansing as the fire—
pray in us.
Hear the silences between our words.
Heal the hurts, the wounds and losses
of those for whom we intercede.
As our lungs and lips breathe in and out,
may our true needs,
deep longings,
unglimpsed hopes,
and paralyzing fears
be exhaled into your heart
through a blessing
sigh.
Amen.

Scripture: Mark 1:29–32

Invitation to Intercession

(*The leader can use his or her own words or some like these.*)
There are many kinds of prayer—prayers of praise, prayers of confession, prayers of thanksgiving. I've chosen for us to pray a prayer of intercession. Some of these prayer concerns may touch the needs of your heart, some may reflect the concerns of people dear to you, and some may be the issues of strangers, and yet we share them together. Just as in this passage from Mark, Jesus healed Simon Peter's mother-in-law, his hostess, the one whose illness touched him closely, he also, after the Sabbath sundown, healed many others who were sick with diseases and filled with demons.

We will share three series of intercessory prayer in this fashion. One of you will read a series of intercessions which will be followed by a verse of "Amazing Grace." Please speak out softly the names of anyone you wish lifted up for any one of the preceding concerns during the singing. Feel free to pray names simultaneously so that we will hear blending with the music an indistinct murmuring of the names. We will conclude each section with a unison prayer, and then the prayer leader will read the next series of intercessions.

Intercessions

For those who live with cancer . . .
For those who live with loneliness . . .
For those who live with addictions . . .
For those who have colds and flus . . .
For those who live with fearfulness and doubt . . .

Hymn: "Amazing Grace"

Amazing grace, how sweet the sound,
that saved a wretch like me!
I once was lost, but now am found,
was bound but now I'm free.

Prayer

For all of these, your children,
we pray for healing, hope, and peace
through Christ our Savior. Amen.

Intercessions

For those who have vision or hearing loss . . .
For those who are HIV positive . . .
For those who have attempted suicide or are close to those who
    have done so . . .
For those whose personal relationships are in transition . . .
For those who have eating disorders . . .

Hymn: "Amazing Grace"

'Twas grace that taught my heart to fear,
and grace my fears relieved;
How precious did that grace appear
the hour I first believed.

Prayer

For all these, your children,
we pray for healing, hope, and peace
through Christ our Savior. Amen.

Intercessions

For those who are recovering from heart attacks . . .
For those who are recovering from disappointments . . .
For those who are living with mental illnesses . . .
For those who are living with grief . . .
For those who are marked by domestic violence or incest . . .
For all of those who are marked by traffic accidents . . .
For all who need healing . . .

Hymn: "Amazing Grace"

Through many dangers, toils, and snares,
I have already come;
'Tis grace has brought me safe thus far,
and grace will lead me home.

(*Unison*) For all these, your children,
we pray for healing, hope, and peace
through Christ our Savior. Amen.

Scripture: Matthew 9:18–26

(*This invitation can be phrased in the leader's words.*)
Jesus interrupted a miracle to heal a woman who had been ill for many years. But she was the one who reached out her hand to touch his garment. Jesus often walks through our lives wearing the garments of those we see all the time. As a symbol of *seeking* some healing in our lives, let each of us go to one of the coats that are hanging around the room (*name what the coats are*) and touch them, praying for our own spiritual, emotional, and physical healing as we sing the last two verses of "Amazing Grace" and listen to the benediction.

Hymn: "Amazing Grace"

My God has promised good to me,
whose word my hope secures;
God will my shield and portion be
as long as life endures.

When we've been there ten thousand years,
bright shining as the sun,
We've no less days to sing God's praise
than when we'd first begun.

Benediction

May the Creator, who loves us into being—
body, soul, heart, mind,
and the Christ who loves us into grace—
forgiveness and compassion,
courage and cross,
and the Spirit who loves us into blessings—
prayer and healing,
hope and new words
tenderly keep us all our days.
Amen.

Please take home the scrap of fabric from your bulletin as a reminder of this service or as a gift to someone for whom you prayed today.

prayers of young people

HEALING AND HOPING

God is like a marble, always moving place to place, with some scratches and dents—not perfect. Each scratch or dent is like a scar, remembering all the things which have happened in this not-perfected world. Each dent reminds God of each person given luck or hope. Like the marble, God, always moving, always rolling, never stopping, never weary, gives help to anyone who ever needs it.

Erin Dezell

Dear God, I pray that all paralyzed people should not be picked on. They are just like other people and they have the same feelings. I pray for healing for many people and especially that people should understand the feelings of others. Amen.

Mike Gavard

Dear God, I will pray for the people with AIDS and wear a red ribbon. I will write a loving song for those who are suffering with HIV. Dear God, please care for all people whom AIDS has touched. Help them live with their pain and sorrow. Amen.

Kelly Pleva

Dear God, please help the children who are abused in any way. At their age they have no way to defend themselves against abuse. Also please help children who are abandoned by their parents and those who have diseases which will kill them. Please let them be alive for a little while. And young girls who are pregnant or already have children, please help them. They have too many hard decisions so early. People have the right to be safe and to be able to live. Amen.

Danielle Pendleton

Almighty God, who watches over us both day and night, to you I pray. I pray for the horses called Tennessee walking horses. What the breeders do to those horses is monstrous. Some breeders drive nails into the hooves of these horses so that they pick their feet up high because it hurts so much. Others wrap their horses' legs so tight that the horses' circulation is cut off. This also hurts the horses' legs so that they lift their feet up in pain. To make their horses' tails look very high, the breeders break the horses' tails and stand them high. I pray for these horses with all my might. Amen.

Ariel Conant

Prayer for Anxiety

I know, God, that I will feel the air grow thick around me again. I know my muscles will tighten, tremor, and fail. The drumming of my heart will once again deafen me. Its pounding, along with my labored breaths, will push me further into my own despair. I will lie there balled up and crying, feeling alone. Please, Lord, don't let me be alone. Hold me in your arms until I have stopped shaking. Stay by me until I can go on once more. Please remind me that everything is going to be okay, and hold my hand until morning. Amen.

Leslie Hoffman

Why Me, God?

I am 21 years old and have a disease known as chronic fatigue immune dysfunction syndrome. This is some of what I have written about having that disease; it is mostly a prayer to God. And having faith is one of the most important things when you have an illness.

Why me, dear God? Why did this happen to me? Why did I get sick? Why so young? Why did the doctors not believe me? Why were they mean to me? Why did my friends leave me? Why does the pain hurt so badly? Why do I have a disease people don't understand? God, why don't they think about what it would feel like if they were sick? Or that they hurt people when they say horrible things? Why do I feel so old and so young at the same time? Why do I feel like a little girl sometimes and an adult other times? Why do bad things happen? Why do people get sick? Why do kids, like me, have to get sick? Why couldn't I graduate from high school like others my age? Why couldn't I have a pretty dress and go to the prom? Why do I have seizures that torture me and won't go away? Why are the doctors so mean? Why did I have to go to the hospital? Why do people tell me I don't look sick when I feel horrible? Why is the world so mean? Why did the world forget me?

I used to ask those questions all the time, and I won't fool you, I STILL ask those questions. But I'm not going to have answers to those. What I do know is that I have learned so much. What is really important in life. I've learned we must always have faith even when we can only see a tiny bit of light or none at all. God is always there. Faith, hope, and love are always there. If we reach for them. Love is the greatest gift God gives us. And even sick or with problems, we can still share our love.

Why me, dear God? Why did you create me? Why do you love me so much? Why did you send Jesus for my sins? Why did you give me such a loving family? Why did you give me a mother who understands and goes through this disease with me? One who advocates for me, when I cannot myself? Why did you finally give me such understanding doctors? Not only ones who understand and listen, but also really care about me. Why, God? Why did you create such beautiful music that helps me to deal with feeling so sick all the time? Why have you given me the chance to learn what most people never learn? Why did you give me the chance to be your Light and to help others? To love them? Why do you love me so much, dear God?

Love, Your Servant,

Rebecca Ann Duger

You never think that a tragedy would happen in your family, at least I never did. Everything happens to other families, and car accidents are only things that happen to people who drive badly. You see, the story I have to tell is one you might have heard on the 5 o'clock news on May 26, 1998, and it may have been just another news report that you think about for only a few seconds, and then say to yourself, "Oh, I feel so bad for that family," and then you might never think of it again.

It was the day after Memorial Day and I was at home getting ready to go to the high school baccalaureate. I was playing in the band and singing in the chorus, and was very excited. I had talked to my mom about 3 o'clock that afternoon. The conversation, though nothing out of the ordinary, is one I will always remember. I ended with a simple "I love you" and, "See you when you get home." Around 5 o'clock, I began to get a little annoyed because my mom still wasn't home. I cooked dinner and, while I was outside, someone called from the Concord Hospital, but that didn't seem unusual, because my mom works there. We didn't even think about it until half an hour later the phone rang again. My dad answered the phone. "Hello, is this Michael Snider?" The woman went on, "This is your wife's boss, and I'm sorry to inform you that Mary has been in a terrible car accident. She has a broken arm, collapsed lung, and other severe injuries."

I was so shocked, I didn't know what to say. This wasn't something that could happen to my family. It didn't seem real at first. My dad made me go to the baccalaureate ceremony. I didn't want to go, but in the long run I think it was best. I was very upset all through the ceremony, but my friends Elizabeth, Margaret Nolan, and Jonathan were there to help raise my spirits. I was glad afterwards, too, because I didn't want to see my mom in an emergency room. I thought I was prepared for what I would see when I got to the ICU unit at the hospital, but I was not. You always think of your mom as your protector from the world, but when something like this happens, you wish that you could somehow help her, but you can't.

All you can do is pray for a miracle. So I did.

Jessica Snider

Gentle God, your confused child pleads for advice and forgiveness. Today I was walking home from school with my best friend and some of her friends. I was almost home when her friends pulled out a pack of cigarettes. When they offered me one, I panicked. I didn't want to look stupid, so I took it and had several puffs. The first puff was awkward and I coughed, but as I inhaled more, I started to like it. I've heard about nicotine addiction and the things that happen to people who smoke, and I don't want that to happen to me. You've always been able to help me and answer questions when I need advice. If it's not a sign you give me, it's a feeling. So, I'm asking you now—what should I do? Amen.

Liana Merrill

Dear God,

Are you there? Can I talk to you a minute? I need some advice and your opinion means a lot to me. I'm worried. I don't know how to deal.

My friend is [doing drugs*]. His/her grades are going down. S/he's moody; his/her parents are mad at him/her but they don't know what's going on. My friend doesn't care about anything but his/her drugs.

We're losing our friendship; s/he's not what s/he used to be. I need you to help me help my friend.

What do I do? How do I get through to him/her? Should I be staying friends? Who could I tell? Who could help?

I read in the Bible about miracles, but when I pray, nothing big happens. But still, I'm kinda like hoping. . . . If you're listening, please help me out. Thank you.

*We have experienced different concerns for our friends regarding risky behavior. We decided to focus on one (drug use), but other substance abuses and eating disorders raised similar anxieties for us. We encourage people to substitute whatever worrying behavior your friend might be engaged in.

Pilgrim Congregational Church, UCC, Lexington, Massachusetts
Jennifer Armstrong, Tim Breton, Bob Litchfield, Sarah Masoner,
Sarah Murphy, T. J. Porter, Jennifer Raymond, Eric Siegel,
Samantha Smith

8 gathering at the table

The prayers collected here focus on table-gathering and, by extension, the community of faith and faith identity. Some focus on the end of Lent/Holy Week time frame. Spring seasonal pieces are found in chapter 11, "Celebrating the Earth."

The activities that follow might be appropriate for a long evening of Lenten vigil. They could take place one an hour, with free time in between, from 8:00 P.M. until 10:00 P.M. with an 11:00 P.M. worship service, or they could be used in any combination. The focus is on table-community, and the evening concludes with a communion service reflecting gratitude for those who have come before in the faith.

YOUTH MINISTRY ACTIVITIES

Taste and See That Our God Is Good

Read Psalm 34:8. On a large tray, perhaps a school cafeteria tray, place food items. Suggestions are Oreos, M&M's, Cheerios, onion slices, raspberries, coffee beans, chocolate chips, popcorn, cotton candy, lemon or lime wedges, garlic. Each participant eats or tastes one of these foods and then writes a prayer, letting that food be the "parable" that sparks it. Let senses, memories, and free imaginations encourage prayers that don't sound "churchy." Share some of these prayers—laugh a little and be touched—then eat up the leftover "good" stuff.

Confession on a Plate

Read Luke 19:5–7, a section of the familiar Zaccheus story, after he comes down from the tree. Pass out paper plates. Invite each young person to write at the center of the plate the category of person with whom he or she would not be comfortable sitting down at the banquet of life (a personal "tax collector") and then to write on the plate a prayer that includes this person. Encourage them not to self-censor their prayers. Some participants will want to read their prayers aloud. After each prayer respond, "This is table-grace."

Temple Turnover

Read Matthew 21:12–13 Going through the sanctuary, turn over (gently, ritually, rather than in anger) everything that can be placed on its side—chairs, communion table, font, candles, music stands, crosses. Even put the Bible on the floor. Look around and see how unnecessary these things are to a house of prayer. Discuss the feelings the young people would have if Jesus came in and did this in their sanctuary. Take a few photographs of the disorder to share with the deacons of the church.

What Lights the Church?

Try to collect at least three times as many votive candles as participants. Put them, unlit, in the middle of the nave carpet and sit around them. Going around the circle clockwise ask each young person to light a candle and say, "_____ lights the church." Then each one should take the lit candle to a symbolic place. (For example, the candle representing "music" on top of the organ, "children" or "people" or "friends" in the pews, "the Bible" on the lectern, "money" in the offering plates.) When all the candles have been lit and the group has stretched their collective imagination, go to a vantage point (balcony?) to see how beautiful this is. Contrast this with the temple turnover and take another photograph to share with the deacons.

WORSHIP SERVICE

Set the table to remember Passover with contemporary "fast food"—a bun in a McDonald's bag, a corn tortilla in Taco Bell wrapping, and some local take-out bread, perhaps a bagel from a local bagelry or a muffin from a bakery. Use the wrappers decoratively so that the point of the Exodus scripture is made visually. Central in the table should be a large size bell (clean!) and a pitcher with juice, but no communion chalice.

Scripture: Exodus 12:11

Take ten minutes of silence reflecting on this passage. You may wish to read more of the Passover story, and make sure that the group knows the connection of Jesus' meal in the Upper Room with the Passover celebration.

Scripture: Luke 17:11–19

Remembering the bell-ringing that lepers did to warn people of their approach and the return of the thankful Samaritan leper, use the bell for a time of Eucharist—of thanks-giving. (Explain that is the definition of "Eucharist" for those who may not know.) Pass the bell around the circle. Each young person will ring it and tell a story of thanks—it may be thanks to God, thanks for an event or for a talent, or thanks for a person who has been a saint, mentor, or healer.

Scripture: Mark 14:22–25

Invitation to Eucharist

We are invited by the Passover story—
with its hurry and holiness.
We are invited by the Passion story—
with its betrayal, denial, and

Roman crucifixion, and the
remembering in bread and cup
that Jesus used
to keep it in our minds always.

We are invited by Eucharist stories,
throughout the years—
from communities of faith
gathered in catacombs, cathedrals,
and around campsites, and
from communities around the world
who share a supper of
wheat loaf, paper-thin host,
rice cake or tortilla.

Prayer of Consecration

God, enter with your wild and holy truth
into this Eucharist of joy—
that it may become your presence in us.
>   Break us like love.
>   Pour us out like healing.
>   Risen Savior, live in us,
>   that we may live in you. Amen.

Pass the bread, saying—
"This is the time to hurry into love."

Invite the participants to hold the bread.
Ring the bell and then turn it upside down and pour the juice or wine
into it.
Pass the bell which is now a cup, saying,

"Eucharist—we give thanks for grace."

Receive communion by intinction.

Prayer of Thanksgiving

God, we thank you for words we taste,
and bread we hear,
and for the cup in which we drink
>   metaphor and mystery,
>   healing and haste,
>   the gratitude of our spirits
>   and a blessing on our lives. Amen.

prayers of young people

GATHERING AT THE TABLE

Dear God, we thank you for all this food set before us. We pray for all the people on the earth who are less fortunate than we are. And help hospital patients who need your special care. Amen.

Brittany Wilson

I thank God for food, family, and friends.
God's been so nice to me.
Each night I pray for guidance
through my life,
And I thank God for everything—
all good things
for my family and friends.
Amen.

Cassie Spencer

Dear God, for all the little moments, I thank you. When I see the blossoms on our apple tree in the spring, I thank you for their beauty. In my childhood, I spent four summer days on my uncle's sailboat. It was glorious weather. At Thanksgiving we go to my grandmother's house and for dessert we have pumpkin pie in front of the fireplace. Each of these simple pleasures reminds me of your love. Amen.

Elizabeth Huessy

God, thank you for my grandma's table. I remember every Sunday
having dinner at my grandma's house. She cooked blueberry cobbler,
chicken, soup, turkey, sometimes, and apple pie. I called it soul food.
It smelled and tasted so good, it made me feel warm inside. After we
would eat, Grandma would go sit in her rocking chair. That was the
peaceful time. God, I knew you were there, too. I know you are at
every table, every house, every place. Amen.

Erica White

Sweet Acceptance

My grandmother has waited a week to see us, her children,
A week of card games and dinners mixed with TV soaps
Newspaper clippings and phone calls
Small chores, showers
Things to occupy the time and keep busy this incredible woman,
Almost eighty-seven,
Until the time comes to see her family.

 I reach out and clasp her hand,
Which is still strong after decades of work and pleasure,
And marvel at the immense being that is a monument to—
A lifetime, city spent, of day-in-day-outs,
One child, a husband, and countless people
Strangers to me,
Friends that have slipped into anonymity and those that are
        remembered,
But are found now only in distant phone books, or, more commonly,
Distant cemeteries. This hand, complete with heavy rings
        and unbreakable nails
(Nails which were passed on to my mother but somehow
        skipped me by),
Is something which I am now finding impossible to let go.

Unaware of the inner feelings which toss my emotional stability
    about like so
much confetti,
She smiles at me, and concentrates on our perilous front steps,
Later years having turned the world into an obstacle course
Of badly placed surfaces, carefully maneuvered around.
As her weight passes through her right hand and into my left,
I am engulfed in a cleaner feeling of love than I have felt
For anyone in more time than I can remember.
It is a combination both painful and elegantly comforting,
A mixture of relief and gratefulness that there is someone
    better suited to handle
the confusion of existence,
Someone I can count on as a support in possible times of trouble,
And the fear I will someday grow up, and we will be separated
By unknown distances and endless phone lines.
I will miss her terribly, and just trying to accept the fact that
    that day will come
Leaves me shaken with tears in my eyes, waiting
    for the moment when
I can throw myself into her arms and escape in the fact that
    she knows this,
And carries the knowledge with more dignity than I could muster
    in a hundred
years of courtly training.

Swept back into everyday life by the sound of her voice
    asking me a question,
I answer, and smile back at her, knowing her love
    will echo back to me.

Jessie Bellantone

Dear God, there are so many of us who are lost and confused about
our sexual feelings. Many of us don't know what hurt may be caused
to ourselves, our family members and you, if we give in to temptations. Please, God, help us to sort out our confused emotions, and
watch over us and guide us so that we can be the Christians we are
working hard to be. In your name, I pray. Amen.

Carrie Johnson

Dear God,
Sometimes it seems that the world is cold,
that no one really feels,
at times I need a hand to hold,
and yours is the one that's real.
I know there's anger and wars,
there's killing and shooting, too,
the anger from these people pours
into pain that's hurting you.
Everyone is so intent on seeing what is bad.
They never see all of your good things,
just the ones that make us sad.
And so at times when it does seem
that the world has lost all hope,
I want to turn this world around,
just like I am steering a boat.
For God I know you love us,
and I will always love you.
Amen.

Carolyn D. Moulton

Dear God, help me to become a better Christian. I believe in you, God, and I believe in Jesus and the Holy Spirit; but I still feel like something is missing. I want to follow your ways, God. I want to become a better Christian. I have heard that every time a person calls out your name, it echoes inside. Please help me to listen for that echo. In my heart I want to hear it. Thank you for your love.

Susan Gooden

Dear God,
In our own lives we don't always feel that we are in such a loving and trusting environment as we are in our churches and our camps. We take a chance putting out our love to others, not entirely knowing if it will be returned or even accepted. Using the model of Jesus' life here on earth we try to share our love. Please help us, for we pray through Jesus' name. Amen.

Bill Halvorson

Dear God, thank you for letting people invent music
so we can express our feelings. Amen.

Jeremy Mann

Our Father Is Great

Our Father is great—
God is always there.
I am not afraid.
God's a hero to me,
the key to the realms of glory.
God is above all, guide to us, and
author of commandments.

And without a shadow of doubt,
I will believe
with God at my side,
I can achieve the greatest of deeds.

Justin Kurtz

O God, help us to be grateful for all you have given us. You gave
your only son to die for us. He bled his scarlet blood for us and cast
his shadow across thousands of years to come so that we would
always remember your great love. As lightning pierced the ground
on that Good Friday, so the memory pierces us and we feel your
great mercy. Amen.

Stephanie Erickson

Dear God, please help me through this time of trouble. I follow your teachings and believe in your words. Times are very tough right now and I need your support and guidance! I am lost, and I don't know what to do, so I turn to you, Almighty God! I need you to help me and give me strength. I trust in you, God, I have learned from your teachings and I believe that you will lead me on the right path. Please be with me, God. I know your love is everlasting! Praise God! Amen.

Kevin Charles Finefrock

Dear God, you are beyond the wind and in the clouds.
Please also be in the shadows by our side,
listening,
when we need you. Amen.

Craig Stevens

(A group prayer, phrases combined from oral prayer)

God, I pray for the family of Timmy, that they make it through the loss of their child. I pray for good results in court. Please help me, for my grandmother is alone and sometimes lonely . . . a lot of times lonely. I love you.

Bless Davenport School staff and residents.

I pray to go home, to get back to my family, to be with my family, to get out of placement, to get home without problems, that my family and I can get back together again and live without arguing, that I can talk to my mom again. I pray to do good in school, to be successful, to make it through everything, to get my life straightened out.

I want to make it in the future and be strong when my dad abuses me. I pray that my mom quits smoking. I pray that my great-grandmother gets better. I pray to find the one I love. Please let Joshua stay safe and sound because I haven't seen him in a year and he's the baby's father.

I pray for my child, Frankie, to grow up. I pray for me, learning to have a healthy life. I pray to feel good about myself, to show care and commitment to myself and others. I pray to move on with my life when I go to court.

Life is like a circle, it keeps going and doesn't have an end. Nothing good seems to happen.

I'm also praying; I would like them to be answered.
Amen.

Davenport School, Northern New Hampshire

What Would Jesus Do?

A question, a little saying—
but with so much meaning.
It calls us to do what God wants us to do.
We consider what Jesus would have done
in times of trial and pain,
in times of happiness and sadness.
When we are unsure about the future,
we must ask ourselves this question.
What would Jesus have done?
If someone had fallen in the road,
would he have walked away not caring?
No, he would have helped them, and so should we.
God, help us to realize
what Jesus would do in tough situations
so that we can decide how to do your will.

Elizabeth Waste

Lord, I know how wicked I am;
The times I hurt others, or myself,
When I sadden you with my sin;
Forgive me, please, O Lord.

Lord, I realize I deserve none of what I ask.
I can never rise above my sins;
But You alone can change me and save me
From the insurmountable evil of my sins.

Lord, I ask for you to forgive me,
For my foolish attempts to save myself,
And for when I forget You, and destroy myself
Through the comforts and pleasures of the world.

Lord, I ask for the strength to help others,
When I am weak and afraid.
Even though I've been selfish and disobedient,
At the end of it You are the only hope.

Lord, I thank you for forgiveness of all my sins;
That when my time comes, I will spend eternity
With You, and not with the evil one.
Forgive me, O Lord.

I glorify You, O Lord, for the assurance
You have given me of salvation:
In the form of your son Jesus, who took
The punishment for all my wrongs.

Kevin Stewart

Dear God,
I know you see all my thoughts,
and everything I do,
but somehow,
discussing it with you in words is so much harder.
When I am in the midst of putting down that person,
or laughing at this one,
I never really think of you.
But, once I start to pray
and realize what you saw me do,
the pain cuts like a knife.
I do do good things, God,
things I know you notice,
but you also know the reason why I do them.
So, I admit,
I did go on that trip to see cute guys,
and to keep my friends from leaving me out,
and not to become closer to you.
But I am fifteen, God.
Sometimes I don't know how to act.
When I see grown people fighting,
killing each other,
over the dumbest things,
I wonder how I am supposed to know what I am doing,
when adults don't.
I forget that you hold all the answers,
that, whenever I am lost, I can turn to you.
But, when I do turn to you,
after you have solved my problems,
I feel like I can fly away.
So, God, my prayer for everyone isn't world peace,
or the cure for AIDS or cancer,
or the cure for hate.
My prayer
is that everyone can learn to pray,
to say a prayer deep from their heart,
and to know that you alone, God,
are the only one who can begin to understand what they want.
In your name I pray,
Amen.

Carolyn D. Moulton

9 praying about parents

This chapter is set in the May–June time that the secular calendar designates for Mother's and Father's Days—those holidays that can be beautiful or terribly painful. Issues about parents—loving parents, abusive parents, parents who are ill, parents who divorce or remarry, teenage parenting, communication with parents, gratitude and mixed gratitude for parents—are all very crucial concerns throughout the adolescent years. In collecting materials for this book, more prayers were written and then withdrawn around these concerns than any others. In this chapter are gathered prayers whose central issue is parenting. Both the activity and the worship sections involve writing and discussion and seek to broaden the definition of family.

YOUTH MINISTRY ACTIVITY

Begin with a discussion circle. Number off by ones and twos to create pairs. Each pair responds to the suggestions below. At a bell, the "number ones" move clockwise to the next "number two" partner. If a particular conversation is intense, a young person can skip over the pair still in conversation and go on to the next "number two." These descriptions open up nurture beyond biological parents.

Describe a landscape from your childhood.

Recount a story that is often told about you from a time before your memory.

Describe an elder who has touched your life—this can be a grand-parent, teacher, neighbor, pastor.

Remember a room—a kindergarten classroom, a hospital room, your grandparents' kitchen, church on Christmas Eve, synagogue at Yom Kippur. What data do your "senses" remember?

Share with the group the response that was most significant or the time when, talking with a partner, you felt the most connection.

Next pass out index cards and pencils. Have a large basket containing common household objects. Include these: safety pin, pocket knife, nails, Band-Aid, spoon, masking tape, electric light bulb, shells, birthday cake candles, can opener, scissors, torn greeting card, stones. Have each participant take an object and write this sentence: "This _____ reminds me of my relationship with my parent/s because _____ ."

Share sentences and reflection on what has been learned.

WORSHIP SERVICE—FAMILY STORIES

Preparation. Invite each youth group member to bring a family photo-graph. Encourage them to define "family" in any way—current family, family of origin, historic family (for example, great-grandparents, with a photo from their wedding day in Italy), family of choice. The picture should include several people. Also invite them to bring journal or paper and pen. (The leader should bring extra photographs for the sec-ond portion of this worship gathering.)

Have a simple low table set with a colorful cloth, a single candle burning, and a handheld mirror with a wide surface. Have a basket filled with unwrapped Band-Aids and make sure to use some silly cartoon character strips, as well as the standard beige ones.

Scripture: Matthew 1:1–16

Have each young person write a story or reflection about her or his photograph. It could be remembering the emotions of the occasion or remarking on who is or is not present in the photograph. It could include brief snatches of dialogue. If someone has forgotten a photograph, ask him or her to write about the particular photograph s/he would have brought (not family in general).

After two or three minutes divide into pairs or triads and share pictures and writing.

Scripture: Mark 4:31–35

Lay the photographs out on the table and invite each person to choose a photograph from one of the other pairs or triads, preferably one whose contributor she or he cannot identify. Take five minutes and write again, this time from information experienced directly from looking at the unknown faces, the setting that is shown, the relationships as they appear. This is a "story"; there is no background, just appreciation.

At the conclusion of the writing time, invite any who wish to share what they have written from imagination. Some human stories are based in memory and some take flight through imagination. Through telling both kinds of stories we learn about ourselves and others.

Photographs are images. Arrange the photographs gracefully on the table so that everyone can see all the images. Let them overlap or touch. The leader might pray in words similar to these:

God, bless these photographs and those who have brought them here today. Bless the people in these pictures and bless the people left out of the pictures. May we all be blessed with clear memory, vivid imagination, and the camera of the heart, which sees truth and then lets each one of us choose a focus for ourselves. Amen.

Scripture: Genesis 1:26–27

Pass the basket with Band-Aids. Have each person take one. Pass the mirror around the circle and ask each person to put a Band-Aid on the mirror, silently thinking of some personal wound or hurt. Then have her/him look into the bandaged mirror and say, "I am created in the image of God."

prayers of young people

PRAYING ABOUT PARENTS

Prayer for Fighting Parents

God, they think we don't hear the yelling. They pretend that we don't know what is really happening. They think we don't see the tears or the awful faces or the pain. I know that I alone can't make it better. I know that I can't make them love again. But, God, I pray for their happiness and for peace once again. Please let the fighting end and the healing begin. Please give them, and me, patience, understanding, and love. Amen.

Leslie Hoffman

Dear God, you are the hands of our earth.
Everything is what you are touching.
As the sunset glows, I smile because I am with you.
You care about everyone,
and your power is great enough to embrace us.
I know that you are there for me
and that my mother is, too.
Thank you, dear God.
Amen.

Megan Fairbanks

Dear God, at this time in my life, when there are so many pressures and issues, help my relationship with my parents to be strong and enduring. Help me to understand my parents and my parents to understand me. Let us be able to think about one another's point of view and to talk things out in a loving way, not a hurtful one. Amen.

Kate Spain

God in Heaven, please bless my family and keep them in your loving care, especially my mom, who has been through some rough times. Please guide her down the path of happiness, so that she may have carefree joy in her life. Please watch over me as I grow, and help me to go down the right paths, so that I will be able to live my dreams and be at peace with myself. Please forgive me for the wrongs I have done, for some words I have spoken and the acts I have done, for they have brought me to tears and I feel greatly sorry. Please, God, take care of me, my family, the many people less fortunate, the people who have a lot, the people who are greedy, the people who are kind, the people who don't have homes, and the people who don't have families. God, bless them all and do your best to take care of them. Thanks.

Leah Broida

Dear God, help me to remember the foundation of my childhood in all its fragments. My life is a brick, the broken shards of which can be glued together into a strong whole. I want to be strong. Amen.

Maria I. Tirabassi

Daughter Words

I'm embarrassed by my poems sometimes,
And they are the closest things I come to
Really being me:
Scribbles that almost translate my soul.
I am ashamed to show them to you
who is closest to my heart,
Who handed me life and blood
And watched in joy (and I suppose fear)
As your own cells stopped living in me
And my new mind thought for itself.

You have seen the real me for fifteen years,
You know all my secrets and lies;
My triumphs and failures;
I can hold back nothing from you.
You have seen me at my worst:
Sick, angry, and crying,
With my hair and face a mess,
and you loved me anyway.

I realize that I am shy for the wrong reasons:
I feel that you'll discover all
The lies or exaggerations that I write,
That you'll read of how I mistakenly
Perceive things, and what I think of life,
And instead of being angry you'll be amused.
That you'll see me growing away from you
And instead of holding me back
You'll push me further.
That you will recognize yourself in my
Awkward attempts at growing up,
And you'll clap your hands and laugh.
That instead of crying and holding your baby
Close when she falls, you'll teach her to walk.

Because when I think of you
I don't think of the wild-haired,
Senselessly screaming woman that you sometimes are,
But of a smiling mother with open palms.
Because I know for a fact that no matter how

Bad I am, you will always love me.
Because in the end I am accountable only to myself
And I'm afraid to be in charge;
Afraid to be released,
Afraid to fail.
As I discover myself,
I don't know which I fear more:
Disappointing myself or failing you.

Jessie Bellantone

Dear God, every day I am constantly reminded of your love. It comes in the form of my parents. I constantly test their love for me with my various actions. There are times when I feel as though I should actually lose their love. But I don't. And some days they get so mad at me and vice versa that I am sure my stable family relationships will shake apart. But every day, God, they forgive me and I forgive them. No matter what happens I can feel their love. Their love shows itself to me in all the little things. I thank you for that love—it is your greatest gift to me. Amen.

Jeff Fahrenholz

Dear God, please help me through the hard time in my life. I am a teenage mother – sixteen years old. My son is sixteen months old. I cannot live with him right now, but I love him more than my own life. Can you help me through the path of my life? I love you. Thank you.

Tawnya

Dear God, I pray to you for the joy you have given my friend as she has just given birth to her first child. Please guide her in raising, teaching, and caring for her newborn child as a loving Christian. Please help her when tough times happen along the way, for I know she will need your strength. I give you praise for this glorious miracle. Amen.

Meaghan Maguire

Dear God, I pray for the children who have been orphaned. I hope that they receive new parents, safe homes, and good lives. I hope they live in warmth and safety and feel love. I hope they get a good education like mine so they can be well provided for all their lives. May each one have a healthy life and good times. In Jesus' name, I pray. Amen.

Audrey Crane

Dear God, please help those children who have no parents. I am very thankful that I have nice parents who love me. Some kids don't have parents, or even any people who care about them. Please help them to learn that you will love them anyway. Please also watch over those children whose parents are mean to them. They probably think that they are not worth loving, but they are. Please be like a parent to them as well. Finally, O God, some children just don't know how lucky they are to have wonderful parents. Bless them, too. In Jesus' name I pray. Amen.

Jaime Van Leuven

Dear God, a single egg represents my memories. When I was young, my parents would hide Easter eggs around the house and outside. I was so excited when I finally found one. I pray that those memories always return to me. This egg also reminds me that on Easter Sunday I would dress up with my bonnet on. Hold these precious moments safe. Thank you, God, that I can be a kid again. Amen.

Megan Fairbanks

God, I would like to pray for Scott. He is dropping out of school and his parents are upset. At this point in his life, being a student isn't what he feels he needs to be doing. School just isn't right for him now. I pray that his parents don't see him as a lost cause or question his decision. If leaving school to pursue his dreams is what he needs to do, I pray that his parents are supportive, even behind him every step of the way.

Scott Harlow

Dear God, I hate the way parents abuse little kids. It drives me nuts that little kids have to be afraid to make their parents mad. So, I pray you will try your best to make sure these kids turn out okay, and keep them safe tonight. I hope you can also forgive me for all the bad things I have done. Please watch over all who believe and need help and keep them safe this night. Amen.

Anonymous, Windsor, Colorado

Where Is Everyone?

"A new beginning." What a special title, right? Many people see the new millennium as a new beginning.

However, there is a darker side to that. Take, for instance, Y2K. Everybody thinks all the computers are going to go haywire, bank accounts will be all messed up, and all chaos will erupt!!

But not me. I see 2001 as a chance for hope and transition for the church. How, you ask?

Well, allow me to illustrate for you. When you go to church, what do you see? Pews, hymnals, Bibles, and the pulpit, of course. But you want to know what I see? A gap. A huge, expansive gap. The way I see it, there are two age groups, the elders and the youth. There's nothing in between. In that sense my church is like Wal-Mart, who goes from Halloween right into Christmas. Apparently, Thanksgiving doesn't even exist to these people. And in my church, the parents are like Thanksgiving, which is to say, nonexistent.

Some people don't believe me and say, "No parents? Well, how do they get there then?" How about their "grandparents"? Remember them? The parents of our parents. That's how I get there. Not to mention I live like five hundred yards from the church so it would look kinda bad if I didn't show up.

So later on, you might ask the parents why they weren't in church, their kids were. Now this is one of the most fascinating moments in human behavior, the excuse.

Some common ones I hear are, "I would've, *but* I stayed late at the casino." Or else there's, "I would've, *but* somebody doesn't like me there. He or she says I'm not welcome." "I would have, but, but, but, but, but."

God, I hate that word! I absolutely hate that word when it's used to make an excuse for yourself. As soon as they say that, that person loses all credibility. They no longer have anything interesting to say.

An hour is a relatively small expanse of time when you think about it, isn't it? I only mention it because that's how long my church's services last on Sunday. Is that too much time to devote to your church, one hour?

An hour that could dramatically affect the rest of your life, here and beyond. Yet, some still can't manage to make it. They can't pull themselves away from the casino, the bar, or wherever for an hour on Sunday. Come on.

Some say, "I don't have anything to wear." How about clothes? They have them, don't they? Come as you are, it's not like God won't listen to your prayers unless you're in a suit or your absolute best clothing. He doesn't care what you're wearing, as long as you're there. That's it. As long as you show up, he'll listen.

Some people say, "I can worship at home." I'm sure you can. However, worshiping in church demonstrates to everyone that you have faith in God, and have made the effort to come to His House to praise Him.

So in closing, I believe a new beginning best could be achieved by a thing as simple as attendance. So when you go to church, please, take a buddy. It will help attendance, and the offering. To have a successful "New Beginning" we need to take the church and God more seriously, and ourselves less so. After all, an hour, once a week, isn't a whole heck of a lot, right?

Marcus Lewis

10 saying goodbye

The lives of young people are filled with "goodbyes." There are graduations from eighth grade and high school. There is departure *for* college and military service and departure *from* college and military service. Weddings are times of parting as well as uniting. There are also "goodbyes" which are not chosen but experienced by young people, such as the divorce of parents, the death of a family member, friend, or pet, or a move to another town. Personal relationships are sometimes a roller coaster of going together and breaking up. New possibilities, however exciting, also contain a leavetaking dimension, and often teenagers are urged to welcome the new without being given a chance to honor the sadness of leaving the old. Prayers in this section reflect some of these issues.

YOUTH MINISTRY ACTIVITY

Divide the group into three sections. Each person will take a lunch-size brown paper bag that includes a common item to be used in the skit. Keep the bags closed until after the discussion portion of the Bible study. Humorous objects such as a roll of toilet paper, a garlic clove, a whoopee cushion, a bar of soap, or an old sock can be added to a wide range of household and clothing items.

Scripture: Genesis 32:22–32

Jacob wrestled with an unnamed One (man, angel, God, or demon) by the Jabbock River, One who would not let him hang on, and who in fact hurt him so that he limped for the rest of his life. Jacob received a new name, the name of a chosen people, and a blessing in the dawn before his inevitable encounter with his brother Esau, whom he had cheated and betrayed many years earlier.

Questions:
1. What is one thing you are "wrestling with" right now? Does it have the potential to both hurt you and give you some new identity?
2. List the whole variety of things that people you know struggle with.

Scripture: John 20:11–18

Mary Magdalene went to the garden where she expected to find the corpse of Jesus lying in a tomb borrowed from Joseph of Arimathea. First she thought she saw a stranger, then she recognized Jesus. He would not let her cling to him, but rather sent her off running to share the good news with others.

Questions:
1. What people and things do you/we clutch that you/we should let go?
2. What personal losses have you had?
3. What does the empty tomb of Jesus mean to you?

Scripture: Acts 1:1–11

The disciples spent forty days walking and talking with Jesus after he was raised from the dead. It was very comforting. Then he vanished up into the clouds and suggested that they would soon have a mysterious power to carry on the good news of his life. They were very confused.

Questions:
1. When do you not want to say goodbye?
2. Do you ever think that things were easier when you were younger and did not have as many responsibilities?

After the Bible study each group should create a completely contemporary retelling of the story, using every one of the props in the bags. Perform these lighthearted stories for the other groups. You may want to go into the sanctuary to share the skits and mention that, just as we often act out the Nativity story in both original and contemporary versions at Christmas time, so it is sometimes important to embody other scripture stories as well.

Optional Activity

Have the holiday! If the youth group created the idea of a perfect holiday when discussing holidays in chapter 4 and this is the meeting when young people who have been part of the youth group will be leaving, plan to celebrate your custom-designed holiday as the activity for the meeting.

WORSHIP SERVICE

Cover the table for a worship center with old road maps and tape them under the edges. Include some distant states or countries as well as some closer, more familiar ones. Put a large branch in a bucket or vase of stones as a "prayer tree." Lay out 8½" x 11" sheets of paper, pencils or pens, and a dark marking pen. Put the communion elements inside a small suitcase under the table.

Call to Worship

Pass the large marking pen around and have each person write a synonym for "goodbye" ("see ya," "adios," "catch you later," "farewell," "I'm outa here," etc.) on the map surface.

Invocation

Holy God, in times of both "hello" and "goodbye" we feel you with us. Our lives are filled with endings and hopings, all mixed together, and feelings of loss and excitement which we do not always understand. Teach us how to love one another by waving as well as hugging. Amen.

Scripture: Genesis 32:22–32; John 20:11–18; Acts 1:1–11

Prayer

God, some of us experience rivers of fear and self-doubt.
Some of us experience graveyards where our hopes are buried.
Some of us experience a mountaintop of clouds and happy-sadness.
We are willing to wrestle and weep and say "goodbye."
We expect in all the journeys of our lives
to encounter God, feel hurt, hear our own names, or receive new ones,
and be given the Holy Spirit to guide us on the road. Amen.

Prayer of Intercession

(*Each person takes a piece of paper and a pencil or pen. As the forms of departure are read slowly, followed by a pause, each person writes down the first names of those mentioned.*)
O God, we pray for those who are in the midst of transition:
> for those who are graduating . . .
> for those who are leaving home . . .
> for those who are getting married . . .
> for those who have lost a family member,
>> a friend, or a pet in the last year . . .
> for those who are moving or have moved,
>> or miss someone who has . . .
> for those who are breaking up personal relationships . . .
> for those whose families are touched by divorce . . .
> for those who are going on a foreign exchange program . . .
> for all others who are on the brink of farewell or
>> trying to recover from a departure . . .
God, wrap a benediction around each one of these.
Let the love be felt so deeply that healing and hope
> warm each heart. Bless every "goodbye." Amen.

Fold each sheet of paper into a paper airplane and then tape the planes to the prayer tree.

Holy Communion—"In Our Own Words"

The young people who will finish youth group at the end of the year should lead this communion. This can be planned out and written in advance or spontaneous. A couple of the departing youth group members who do not like to speak in front of others should pull out the suitcase and open it up, revealing the communion elements and then making an "altar" out of the suitcase. There are five speaking parts. Any other departing members should pass the elements.

Invitation (Speaker #1)

We are all invited to the table of God's gifts.
Let me offer this invitation in my own words:
(*The speaker may add a general welcome to the group.*)

Prayer of Consecration (Speaker #2)

Dear God, we offer this bread and this cup and ourselves to be changed into something holy today. Please hear me pray in my own words:

Amen.

Words of Institution—Bread (Speaker #3)

Jesus shared bread with his disciples.
Let me tell you what that means in my own words:

Words of Institution—Cup (Speaker #4)

Jesus took a cup on that last Passover evening and asked us always to do this, remembering him. Let me tell you what that means in my own words:

Prayer of Thanksgiving (Speaker #5)

Holy God, we thank you for this table which is so precious to us. Please accept the thanks I give in my own words:
(*This prayer may include thanks for the youth ministry year, for friends, and for leadership.*) Amen.

Closing

There may be a gift or symbol for departing members, a benediction or a passing of the peace. There should be food and an opportunity for continued casual conversation.

prayers of young people

SAYING GOODBYE

Winds blow and the air grows cold,
minutes click into hours,
days go by and the clock turns,
and the weeks change into years—
This is how we measure the passage of time.
Or is time instead recorded by memories?
Standing with friends and family,
watching as a clock counts down, a ball falls,
cheering and singing as a year ends and another begins;
or perhaps is it that eve, lying in bed,
turning over restlessly, waiting to spring up,
rush down the stairs, and rip asunder the colored papers,
papers hiding gifts given with love.
Is it birthdays that measure time?
Celebrating each year we've been alive,
learning to walk, learning to cry.
Or is it pain that marks our hours?
Moving on, saying goodbye?
Do we know time has elapsed from how long ago someone died?
In pain, in love, with joy and with longing,
we remember the seconds as they speed by.

Jeannine Karr

All through life we walk a road.
It twists and turns along the way.
We meet many people along our journey.
We make friends, get to know one another.
But, like our own, their roads change, too,
and sometimes we must say goodbye.
Sometimes we walk in daytime
sometimes at night.
God is always with us and will
see us through every tomorrow.

Elizabeth Waste

Can you hear the rhythms—
the streams murmur, birds sing, and the sun speaks.
The mountains seem to look upon and protect the wildlife.
Throughout the seasons there are cycles; life arrives
and leaves, but it will be back.
Waves may wash away footprints,
but they will appear again.
Life is.

Justin Koonz

Don't let me fear being lonely. Allow the woods and the river to be my friends, and let me walk in their companionship with gratitude. Amen.

Maria I. Tirabassi

Dear God, please help me be strong while I go through a difficult part of my life. Please let me make the right decisions as I live my life. I know I will be facing a lot of problems in my teenage years. Life is very difficult, and I will look to you to help me. I know I will make my own decisions, but I will look towards you for advice. I am constantly reminded of your love and care. Amen.

Kristy Orr

Dear God, giver of life and creation, please hold a vigil over my friend. She is drifting away, dim and worn, like a faint October leaf. Please help her to understand she is important to me and I am afraid to lose her. I am sorry for being snappy and for my harsh angry words. Help her to hear my apology. Amen.

Gabriele Sarah Chase

Mother Birds

Person I need most
Doesn't mean to hurt. Neither
Do I, but we do.

Once you gave me life,
Now I'm learning to live it.
Thank you, now let me go.

I told you, nervous,
You listened, you understood.
Wait, please, take me back.

You open your arms,
I am free to fly, but now
I hold on tighter.

Is this how mother
Birds feel, pushing weak, nervous
Chicks out of their nests?

Freedom tastes so good,
Longing brings me back and you
Welcome me each time.

Jessie Bellantone

God, as my senior year comes to a close and I venture out on my own to college, I pray that I stay in contact with all of my friends. My friends and I have come to a fork in the road of our friendship. I pray that our journeys do not continue to split further and further apart, but that they run parallel to each other and occasionally cross paths. Maybe I won't see them tomorrow or the next day, but I hope that my leaving will not be a "goodbye" but a "see you soon."

Scott Harlow

Thank You

Sarah
My sister
You were always there
Always listening
Always hearing my obnoxious crying
Always comforting me
You were always there to gossip about boys
And sometimes throw me off your bed
And out of your room
You yelled when I came in without knocking
And when I interrupted phone calls with friends
You sang with me when I had a song
You held me when I was sad
You put up with me asking if it was your boyfriend when a boy called
You helped me with problems with friends

And even though you're there and I'm here,
I want to thank you, Sarah, for
all that you've done.

Elizabeth Fineberg-Lombardi

I'm not nearly the first to endure the loss of a friend.
Many unknown to my eyes have felt the void
and recognized the affliction of a broken soul.

I realize others have lit a candle in remembrance,
and seen the tear they swore wouldn't fall
extinguish its fragile warmth.

But I barely remember.

I've visited the grave,
laid flowers upon the headstone
as I'm sure others have before.

I know this to be truth, and yet,
my heart still weeps
with loneliness.

Maria I. Tirabassi

Eternal

Through gentle twilight's
Fierce hello
That bellows sense,
Soft and slow:
Stumbles down to muted ears
(shadowed backdrop to ease the years).
Mindful summit of cherished days
Replaces foreign, younger ways.
Sweetest laughter now
flickers, solemn.
Every
Sunken
Wrinkle
Fallen.
Casement made as forth we cry
Abandoned now
By years gone by.
And we are but babes,
once more—open now,
exposed and sore.
And through the empty, hollow night,
Beyond sweet heaven's
Sodden light
Upon my wings
to tomorrow's past
I lull you, bathe you—

Endless time
at last.

April Kelley

God is like a feather,
floating in the air.
No one notices it there,
But we feel something.
When God watches you
in the form of a feather.
you will know
God is there—
But where?

Kyle Behring

A Good Night Prayer (prayed by me since I was four years old)

Help me be good,
Help me be calm,
Help me be good for Mom and Dad.
Help me be a good sister.
Help me be a good friend.
Help me be kind to animals,
and give me the power.
Amen.

Sayre Wilson

11 celebrating the earth

The natural world comforts and inspires young people, challenges them to grow and become resourceful, and affirms for them the reality of human interconnection with earth, water, sky, and animal and plant life, in spite of the omnipresence of technological culture. Prayers with natural objects as metaphors or parables often reveal deep truths about the lives of adolescents. The prayers in this chapter reflect this, as well as the concerns of ecology— the need for stewardship of resources.

Summer camping programs and weekend youth group trips are often remembered by young people as times of significant encounter with God. Physical experiences in the youth group context such as biking, hiking, canoeing, and skiing are sometimes the only opportunities youth have to enjoy their own bodies outside the arena of competitive athletics, which often dominates school programming. The beauty of inanimate nature—a flower, a rock, a leaf—can be the focus of meditation.

Programming possibilities for celebrating the earth are far-ranging. Given the limitations of one chapter, the activity focuses on the human connection with animals, and the worship centers around places that have been experienced by young people as holy.

YOUTH MINISTRY ACTIVITY—BLESSING THE ANIMALS

Many churches offer services of "Blessing the Animals," but these often focus on pets owned by members and have the wonderful but chaotic dimension of inviting those animals into a worship space. This discussion/activity offers a simpler and more inclusive approach. Young people should be invited to bring a *photograph* of an animal—a current pet, a pet who has died, or any animal that has some significance to the individual. Possibilities include birds at a feeder, wild animals photographed in their own setting, or a magazine photo of an animal that the young person identifies with in some way—almost a totem or alter ego.

Opening Prayer

God, we are surrounded by animals—
We are related to animals, served by them, clothed in silk and wool and leather that they provide. Many of us are fed by animals through milk and eggs and meat. We are companioned by the animals we call pets, and we are entertained by animals—in a zoo, in the sky and country around us, under the water of whale watches and snorkeling. We follow the movements of animals with binoculars and cameras, hunting guns and rods and reels. We are deeply grateful to animals who have given well-being and even life itself in the developing of cures for our illnesses. God, keep us always mindful of your children in feather, fur, and fin. Amen.

Sharing Stories

Invite everyone to share the photograph or picture and a story behind it. Why is this animal meaningful? Create a poster or banner using the pictures to share with the congregation.

Hot Teddy

Issues of animal activism are felt intensely by young people. As an attempt to defuse angry debate but begin to talk about issues, this is a simple game. The group sits in a circle on the ground and passes a teddy bear around with music playing. When the music stops, the person holding the teddy answers the next question. The questions ask for a yes/no answer followed by further explanation. Not answering puts a player out of the circle. Go through the list a couple of times. Try to keep the discussion light and evocative.

1. Would you wear a fur coat?
2. Do you swat mosquitoes?
3. Should animals be used to test cosmetics?
4. Should animals be used in cancer research?
5. Are you / could you be a vegetarian?
6. Could you empty a mouse trap?
7. Do you like to hunt or fish?
8. Would you have a snake as a pet?
9. Do you like the zoo?
10. Would you neuter/spay your pet?

Closing Prayer

God, I thank you that I am an animal, with many senses.
    I thank you for my eyes—
        with eyes I see the world.
    I thank you for my ears—
        with ears I hear music and silence.
    I thank you for my skin—
        with skin I touch everything
            hot and cold, soft and hard,
            wet and dry, rough and smooth.
    I thank you for my tongue—
        with a tongue I taste food and talk,
    I thank you for my nose—
        with a nose I smell
            wind and flower
            and dinner cooking,
        and with my nose I breathe.
    I thank you for my senses—
and for the discovery that one sense
is heightened when another is diminished.

God, I thank you for my life—so full of joy,
and for my body—so full of feelings. Amen.

WORSHIP SERVICE—TAKE OFF YOUR SHOES

Gather around a worship center of several boxes covered by a large cloth, creating a series of steps where shoes will be placed on different levels for a later activity. Put a few candles on the boxes at the beginning.

Scripture: Genesis 28:10–17

(*The leader can reflect upon holy ground in the biblical text. Here is a suggestion.*)

There's a whole map of stories in the Hebrew Bible about holy ground, holy places, where people have paused and rested and felt God's presence. This story about Jacob is a favorite. Jacob was fleeing from his twin brother, Esau, after tricking Esau out of his birthright and stealing his blessing. Jacob ran in fear for his life, running alone and in danger of attack by wild animals. Finally, too exhausted to go a step farther, he lay down with a stone instead of a pillow and had a dream of angels going up and down a ladder to heaven while he was surrounded by the sweet promise that God would be with him wherever he wandered.

Jacob woke in the morning and said, "Surely God is in this place—and I did not know it!" Jacob took the stone and poured oil on it and promised that he would return if God kept him safe.

There are lots of holy ground places in the Bible. My invitation to you now is to think about what has been a holy ground place for you. Just one—one outdoor place where you suddenly realized, "Surely God is in this place and I didn't know it." I invite you to turn and share that story with a neighbor. (Let's echo the church service and call it "passing the *place*.") We'll take about five minutes to share these stories.

Passing the Place

(*Participants talk with each other about their special places.*)

Shared Reflection

Ask for any people who would like to share their places.

Prayer

God, for all the holy places—
where we see stars or wildflowers,
where we touch leaves or sand,

where we listen to birdsong or a seashell,
where we smell pine needles
or taste the wind,
we give you thanks.
For all the places we remember and name,
we thank you and say together:
Surely God is in this place. Amen.

One-Shoe Offertory

You know the Moses story—bulrush rescue, faithful sister, privileged youth, sudden rage, flight, love and marriage in Midian, and then that bush that flamed up and got his attention so he could listen to the amazing call of God. Do you remember that the first thing the bush said to him was, "Take off your shoes, you're standing on holy ground"?

We are going to remember that today. As a symbol of the holiness of *this* time and *this* place where we are together, those who wish may remove one shoe and bring it forward, placing it prayerfully on these steps in our worship center.

Doxology *(sing together)*

Praise God, who sees our journeys through.
Praise God, who maps the darkness, too.
Praise God, who loves us—run or crawl,
And gives us wings when we would fall.

Prayer of Dedication

God, slow us down.
Let us feel the ground and
love it better
for being in touch with it. Amen.

Footprint Sermon

Lay out a roll of white paper and invite everyone to draw around her or his stockinged or bare foot and write in the footprint the name of one place he or she wants to "go" with God. Read off the footprints, each one saying, "I want to go to _____" and the group will respond, Amen.

Benediction: A Stone for a Pillow

Remembering the story about Jacob, give everyone a stone.

May you go forth this night to rest
and dream of a ladder
of angels,
and wherever you journey
may your footprints always walk
on holy ground.

Postlude

Retrieve the shoes by coming forward and taking another person's shoe. Then, in silence, find the owner by looking only at feet.

prayers of young people

CELEBRATING THE EARTH

Thank you, God, for all of the nature around us.
Thank you for the sea,
seashells, starfish, sailboats,
and all the rest of the things in the ocean.

Thank you for the children,
the teenagers, and the adults.

Thank you for the hornets,
the tree frogs, the eagles, the hawks,
the mosquitoes,
and all of the animals.

Thank you for guiding us away from alcohol and drugs,
like heroin and cocaine.

Help us to appreciate the beauty of life.
Amen.

Caitlin Jones-Bamman

Dear Lord,
thank you for everything in this beautiful world:
the ocean shimmering and silvery in the moonlight,
the birds singing in the trees at dawn,
the lilac and the crocus that bloom in springtime,
even the lightning that flashes and glows in the night.

Thank you for the days filled with jubilant laughter,
and all the precious moments of my childhood.

When I am weary, my faith in You
lifts me up.
I am thankful for everything.
Amen.

Brianna Coolbeth

Dear God,
I am very thankful to you for all that you have given me.
The world is such a beautiful place
and I feel honored to be able to live in it.
Every day is a special one
to know that I am able
to live in a world so wonderful.

Laura Skarvinko

My life, O God, is like a seashell. It's hard and tough on the outside.
But underneath, I am really smooth and I believe that means I can
have an easier life. Amen.

Jeffrey Ferguson

Dear God, you let your light shine on all you have created. When I walk in the woods, your light brightens my way. As I pass a river, I feel purified—the Holy Spirit like water washes my soul with love. I am never lonely walking through these woods, for you are always beside me. Your presence surrounds me in the woods on this journey called life. Amen.

Shannon Keeney

With flowers I see spring, a time of joy and happiness. Then the brightness of petals brings the warmth of summer to my heart. In a field of wildflowers blooming, I imagine the sea of God's children. But every flower is individual, no two alike, each beautiful and unique in its own special way. Flowers are like the human race—all different, all alike.

Kathy Garlo

God, I take solace where I find it. I am lonely and I need a friend. I have found a peaceful retreat. Walking here in the woods, I am calm. A sparkling river gives me hope for a new tomorrow. Amen.

Gabriele Sarah Chase

God is like tree bark because, like bark, God lives in a cycle. Bark grows on a tree, peels off, falls on the ground, and becomes fertilizer for the next tree. Bark lives forever in different forms and God lives forever in different ways at different times in our hearts. God is always with you.

Elizabeth Belote

O God, my body is walking through the woods, but my soul is lonely and feels as cold as a river. Amen.

Andrew Gould

I walk to the lake, quietly listening.
I look at the water, wavy, glistening.
The wind on my face can be sharp,
and, blowing through trees, it sounds like a harp.
There is my shadow, almost always behind.
It holds my soul, which I cannot find.
Yet I know I will travel to there and beyond.
Because of God and heaven I am very fond.

Marcy Lombard

Help the endangered lives. We need them to keep the world beautiful. We need many varieties of plant life, animal life, and human life. Life is precious to all God's creatures, and we need to take care of it so that future generations may experience earth's diversities. We hold so much of life in the grasp of our human hands, but some people don't care if we let go. I need your help, dear God, to hold on. Amen.

Rebecca Hartson

I think we take God for granted, like we do food. God plants seeds in us, in hopes that we will blossom into good people. As a fruit comes from a flower, God helps us to bloom and turn into something wonderful. If God were a tree, we would be the fruit of God's labor. An apple is a form for the seeds as we are for God. An apple is red, and the Chinese believe that red is good and God is good. Apples grow in a lot of places and people believe in God in a lot of places. Underneath the tough skin of differing religions, God is always sweet and forgiving and loving.

Emily Hurst

Dear God, thanks for this wonderful March day,
and for all the children that I see flying their kites. Amen.

Casey Purinton

On Spring

When the rain is pouring down
And all the skies are gray,
Just think upon the dawn
Of the next sun-dried day.

Think on what will rise
From the earth, soft and wet,
That nature, by surprise,
Hath drowned with her sweat.

Up from the earth,
A rose will blossom full,
Showing all the birth
That the land will then fulfill.

Adam Kernander

Dear God, thank you for getting all of us to camp safely. God, please
make this week a great one. Thank you for bringing old friends
together and thank you for bringing new friends together. Thank you,
God, for all the things in this forest playground of yours. Thank you,
God, for the warm love you give to all of us. In Christ's name we
pray. Amen.

Josh Walden

On Summer

The flowers on the trees are soon to fall,
And in their place, leaves of green.
When the colors fade and the beauty stalls,
Replaced is it soon to be.

For the flowers wilt, and fade away,
To make room for the springtime's wife.
And, with the dawning of a new day,
Summer then begins her life.

Adam Kernander

New Hampshire

I agree that this place is as my dad says—
with the rolling mountains that seem to go on for miles,
and the sun shining through the clouds, making all of us smile,
the beautiful colored trees in fall,
and pine trees standing nice and tall,
the snow falling gracefully, the rain beating down,
the crocuses and other flowers rising up all around,
the sap buckets hanging from trees,
and the wonderful honey, fresh from the bees,
the grass nice and green,
and butterflies and ladybugs everywhere to be seen,
the beautiful sunsets,
the breathtaking views,
the wonderful old houses,
the sky so blue.
So I shake my head and agree with my dad—
for surely this must be so—
what other place could be so beautiful?
It's God's country high and low.

Tyler Martin

The Transformation

The sky unveils her face with an undying wrath
That blankets all the land in water.
And from this most natural and violent bath
Life shall forever the more prosper.

Down from the sky nature sheds her tears,
And doing so drastically changes the land.
This outburst immediately ends the fears
That have been impressed on her awakening hands.

Up from the wet there sprouts a tree.
A magnolia that of the sugar called.
And this sprout, such as a deity,
Shall live through nature's crying, all.

Adam Kernander

Insufferable time
That clings—
Eternally foreboding
With caustic memories
The eternal blanket to a
Blackened sky
Submerged.
Unthinkable, without,
Bears unnoticed sprouting,
Blossoms unseen, undetected . . .
Until gossamer petals kiss the sky
Dissolving somber clouds
Into fertile rain.

April Kelley

Dandelion Babies

alone, in self, in hiding,
amidst the roar of white nothingness that
surrounds her being
she sits and watches the cloud of
dandelion children whirl around her quiet
form,
their tiny feather bodies a whisper of
fallen maybes and buried discussions,
future heartaches never to be lived
through, but certainly to be felt
every day, endless days
even after they've landed her on damp
earth
to be buried under shovelfuls of reason . . .

justification cloaks her,
the one garment that still fits
it covers her aching arms and shivering
belly as she waits
watching as the dandelion babies bloom
into the brightest yellow she has ever
seen,
unwanted by so many people, she finds
them beautiful
and cherishes each one, gathering their
soft wildness in her arms
over and over again until her fingers are
stained, piles rest at her feet,
and she has enough to satisfy her hungry
soul.

famished, she forages for food
overturning stones and rotting branches
she discovers nests of insects but leaves
them alone, finding instead
the last of the autumn berries,
she picks handfuls of them and lifts them
to her mouth, savoring their juices
not caring if they dribble down her chin
to stain her coverings,

she didn't like those clothes anyway, not
the guilt that came with them
nor the way they made her feel when she
wore them,
like she ought to be ashamed of her own
skin.

suddenly angry, she tears at the fabric,
pulling and ripping until she can feel the
breeze between her legs and the
sunlight on her back,
satisfaction her only garment.
content now, she finds her way back to
the pile of dandelions
and weaves their slightly wilted bodies
together,
flower after flower, life after fading life,
until the last stem has been used and she
unfolds herself
from her seat on the ground and stands
up, looking down at her creation.

each flower, each useless weed is woven
together to form a new cloak,
and she picks it up and places it around
her shoulder,
pulling her arms through the sleeves and
letting the folds fall around her legs.
laughing, she starts to walk, and as she
walks she notices
new flowers poking through the grass.
a wind begins to blow, and she feels
something dance against her hand.
she looks down, and smiles to herself
as a wave of dandelion babies float into
the air.

Jessie Bellantone